GRAPHIC LIBRARY™

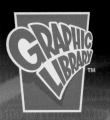

GRAPHIC SCIENCE

THE BASICS OF CELL LIFE

WITH MAX AXIOM™ SUPER SCIENTIST

4D An Augmented Reading Science Experience

by Amber J. Keyser, PhD | illustrated by Cynthia Martin and Barbara Schulz

Consultant:
Monte Westerfield, PhD
Professor of Biology
University of Oregon, Eugene

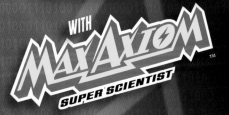

CAPSTONE PRESS
a capstone imprint

Graphic Library is published by Capstone Press,
1710 Roe Crest Drive, North Mankato, Minnesota 56003.
www.mycapstone.com

Library of Congress Cataloging-in-Publication Data is available on the Library of Congress website.

ISBN: 978-1-5435-5875-3 (library binding)
ISBN: 978-1-5435-6030-5 (paperback)
ISBN: 978-1-5435-5885-2 (eBook PDF)

Summary: In graphic novel format, follows the adventures of Max Axiom
as he explains the science behind cell life.

Designer
Alison Thiele

Cover Colorist
Krista Ward

Editor
Lori Shores

Cover Artist
Tod G. Smith

Colorist
Matt Webb

Photo Credits
Capstone Studio: Karon Dubke, 29, back cover

1. Ask an adult to download the app.  Capstone 4D Education

2. Scan any page with the star.

3. Enjoy your cool stuff!

—— OR ——

Use this password at capstone4D.com

cell.58753

Printed in the United States of America.
PA48

TABLE OF CONTENTS

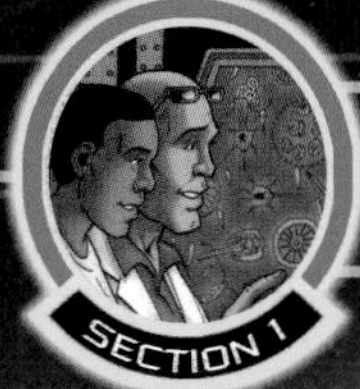
SECTION 1

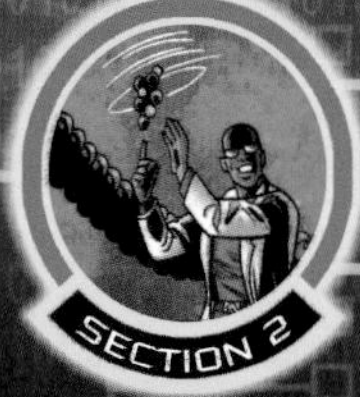
SECTION 2

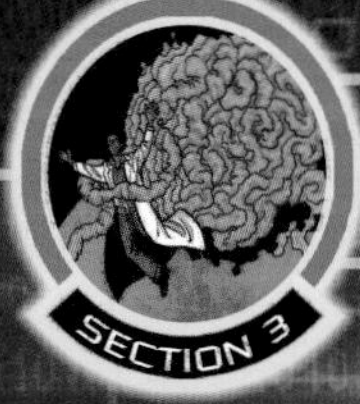
SECTION 3

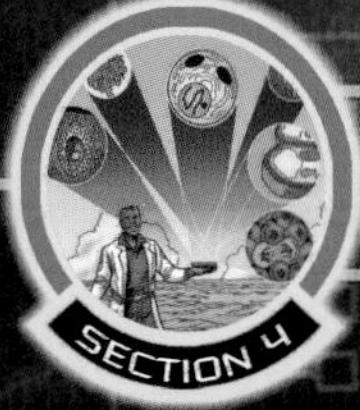
SECTION 4

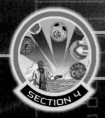

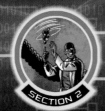

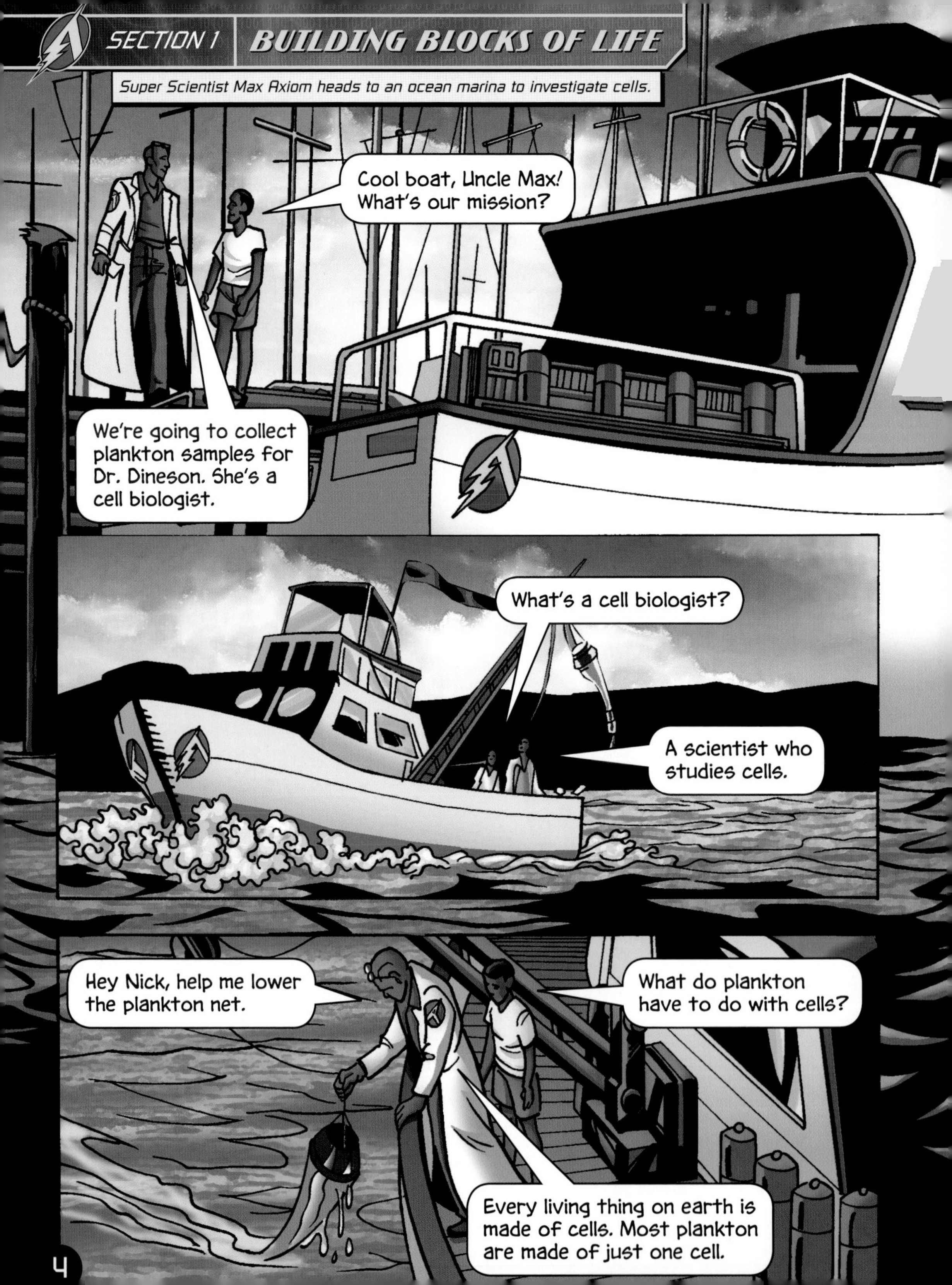
SECTION 1
BUILDING BLOCKS OF LIFE
Super Scientist Max Axiom heads to an ocean marina to investigate cells.
Cool boat, Uncle Max! What's our mission?
We're going to collect plankton samples for Dr. Dineson. She's a cell biologist.
What's a cell biologist?
A scientist who studies cells.
Hey Nick, help me lower the plankton net.
What do plankton have to do with cells?
Every living thing on earth is made of cells. Most plankton are made of just one cell.

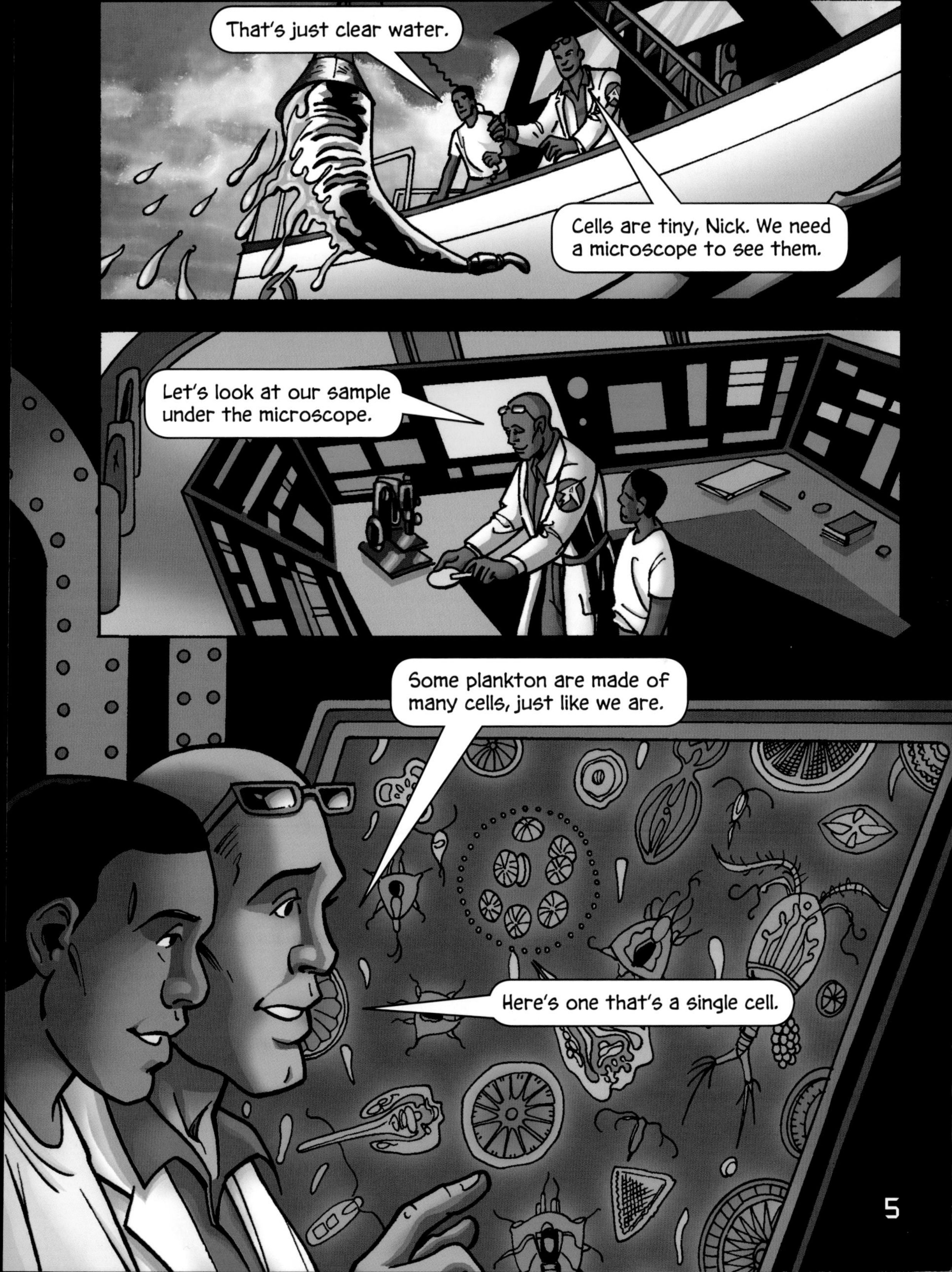
That's just clear water.
Cells are tiny, Nick. We need a microscope to see them.
Let's look at our sample under the microscope.
Some plankton are made of many cells, just like we are.
Here's one that's a single cell.

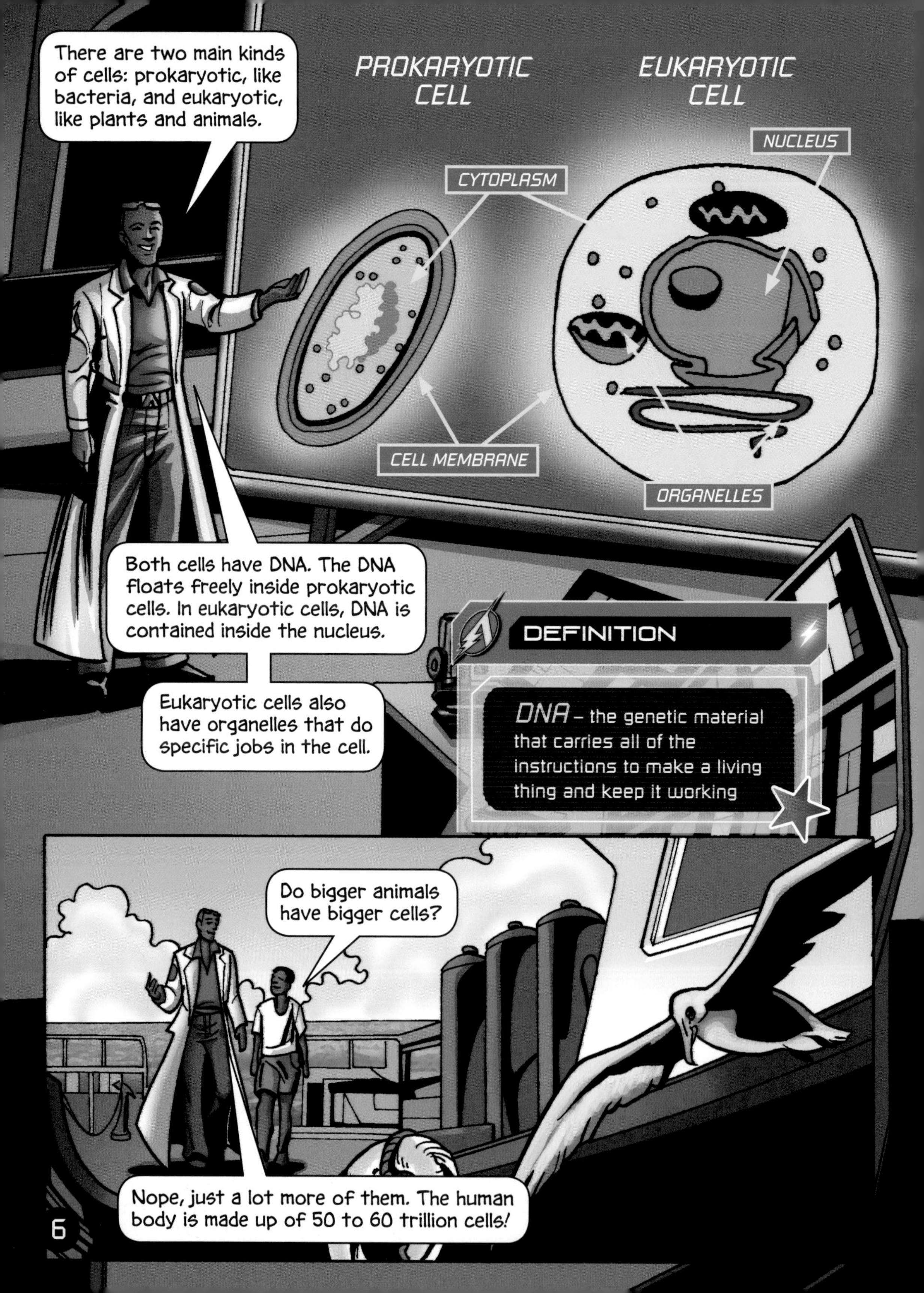

There are two main kinds of cells: prokaryotic, like bacteria, and eukaryotic, like plants and animals.
PROKARYOTIC CELL
EUKARYOTIC CELL
NUCLEUS
CYTOPLASM
CELL MEMBRANE
ORGANELLES
Both cells have DNA. The DNA floats freely inside prokaryotic cells. In eukaryotic cells, DNA is contained inside the nucleus.
Eukaryotic cells also have organelles that do specific jobs in the cell.
DEFINITION
DNA – the genetic material that carries all of the instructions to make a living thing and keep it working
Do bigger animals have bigger cells?
Nope, just a lot more of them. The human body is made up of 50 to 60 trillion cells!

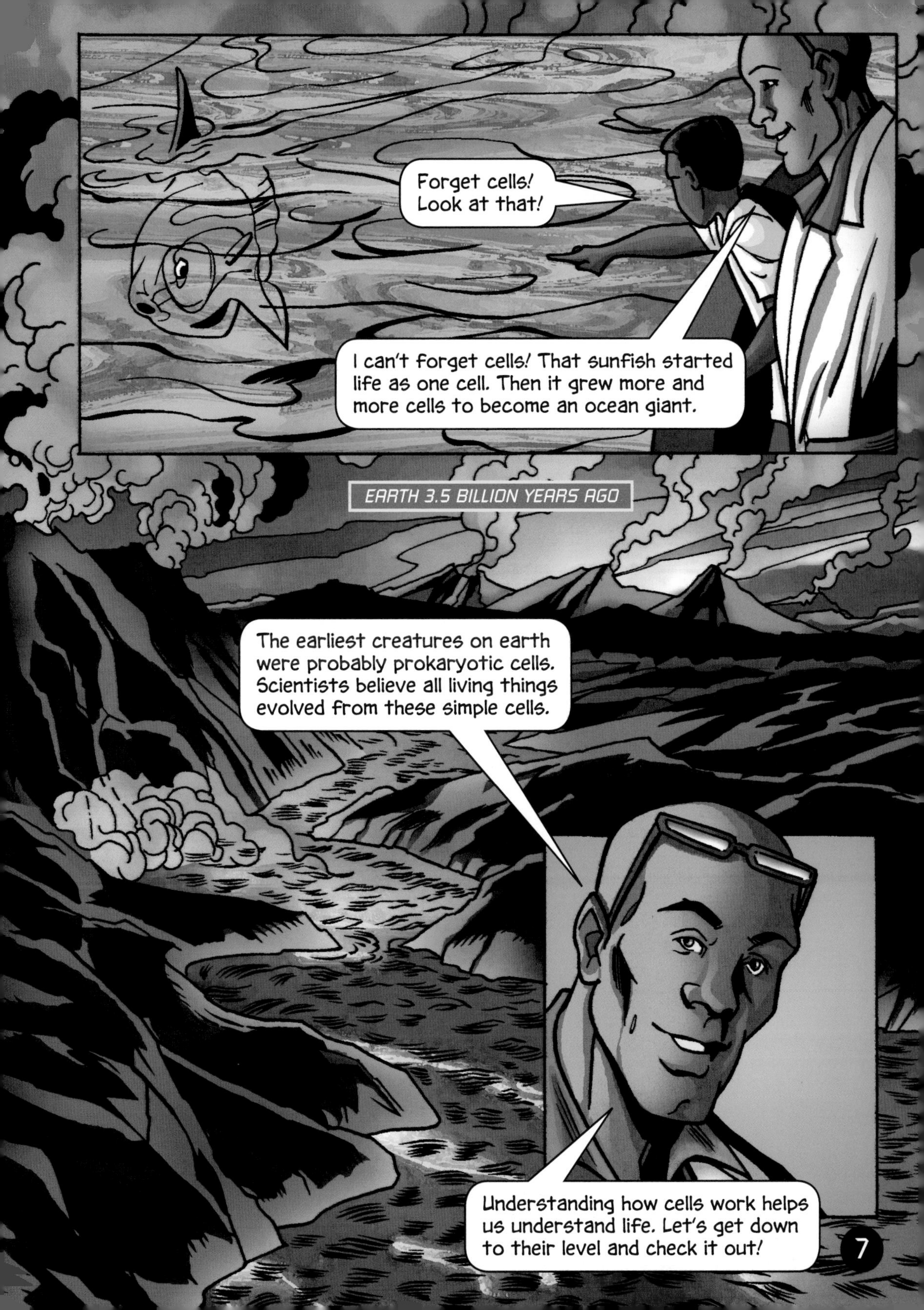
Forget cells! Look at that!
I can't forget cells! That sunfish started life as one cell. Then it grew more and more cells to become an ocean giant.
EARTH 3.5 BILLION YEARS AGO
The earliest creatures on earth were probably prokaryotic cells. Scientists believe all living things evolved from these simple cells.
Understanding how cells work helps us understand life. Let's get down to their level and check it out!

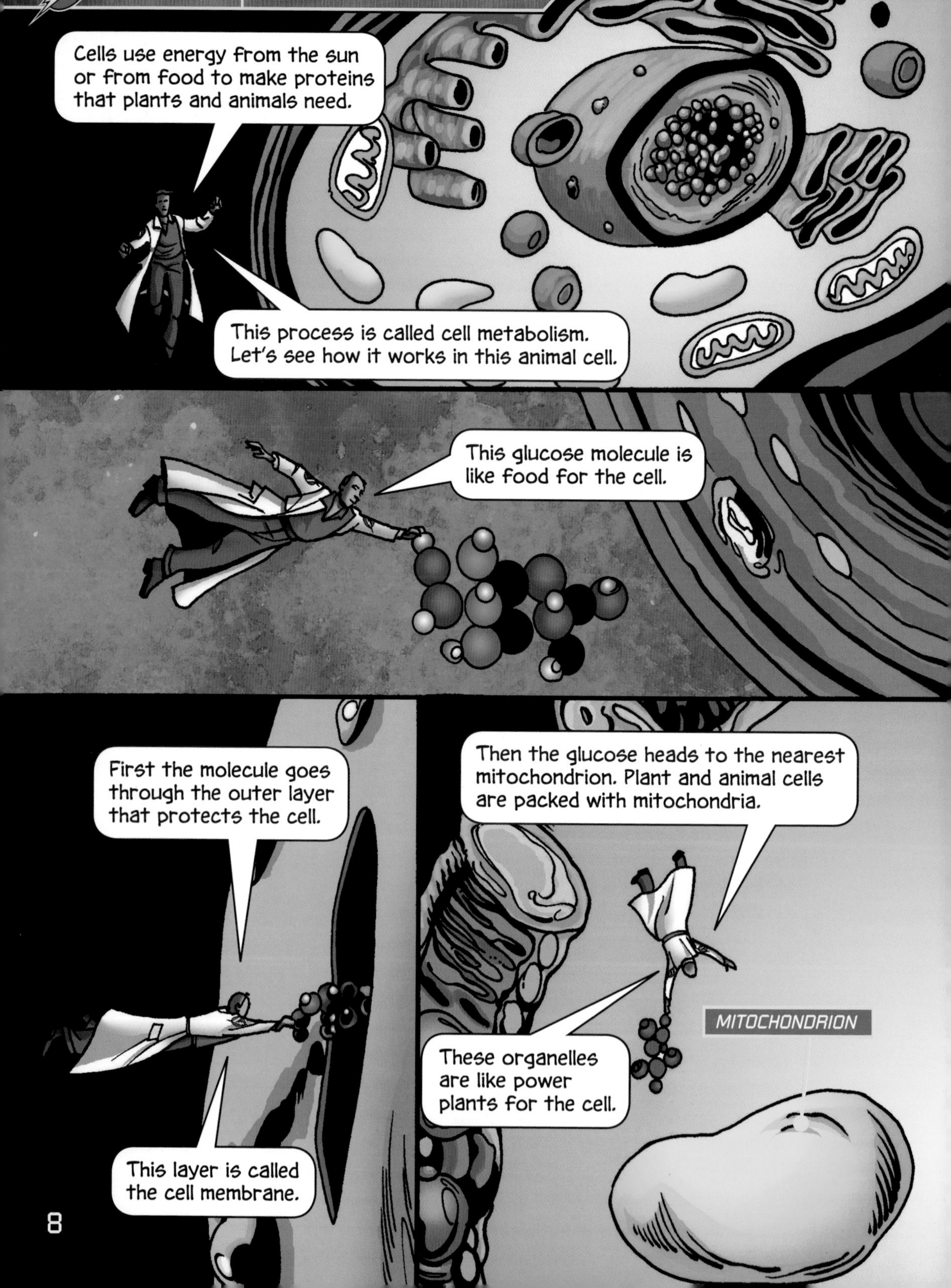
Cells use energy from the sun or from food to make proteins that plants and animals need.
This process is called cell metabolism. Let's see how it works in this animal cell.
This glucose molecule is like food for the cell.
First the molecule goes through the outer layer that protects the cell.
This layer is called the cell membrane.
Then the glucose heads to the nearest mitochondrion. Plant and animal cells are packed with mitochondria.
These organelles are like power plants for the cell.
MITOCHONDRION

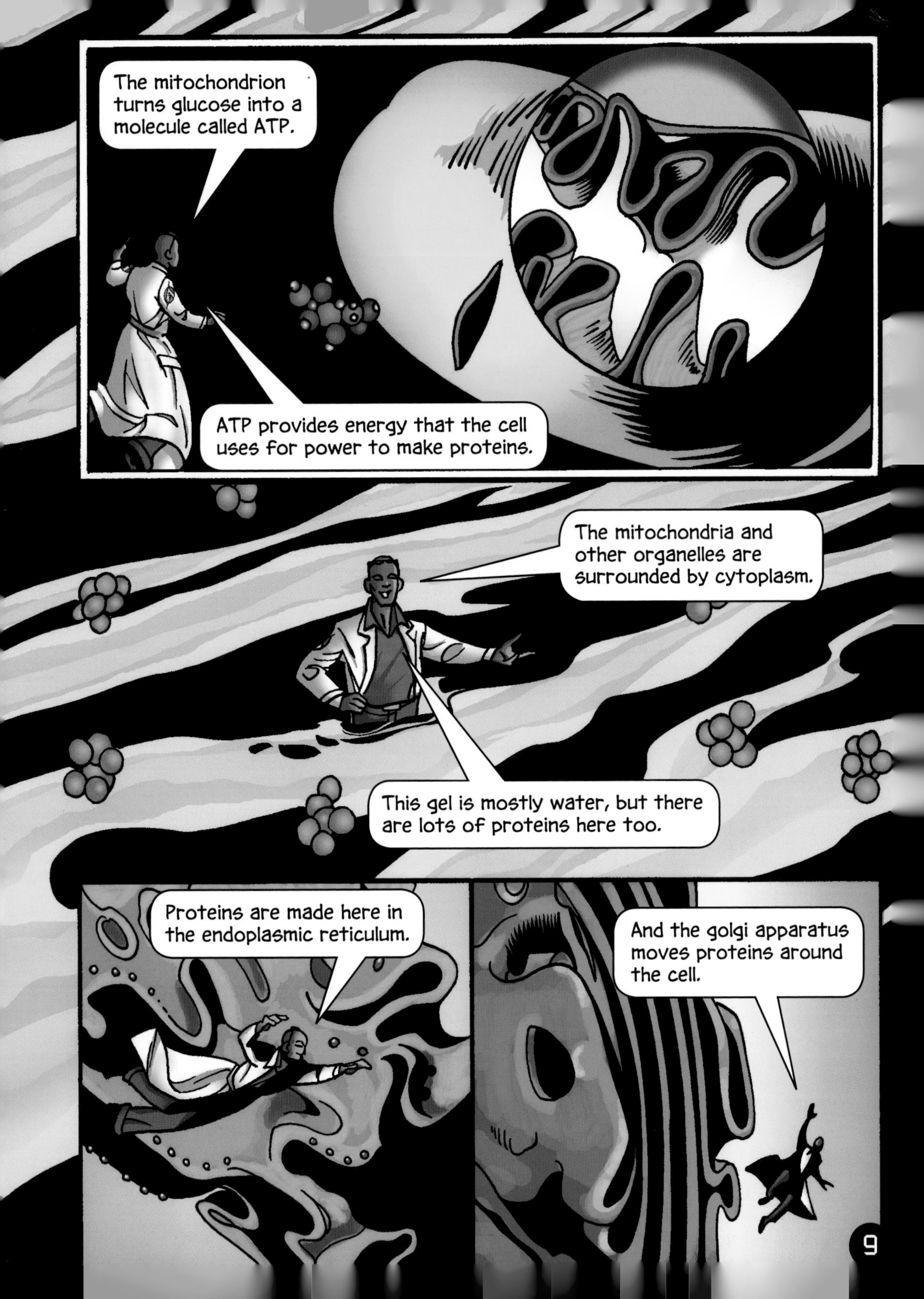
The mitochondrion turns glucose into a molecule called ATP.
ATP provides energy that the cell uses for power to make proteins.
The mitochondria and other organelles are surrounded by cytoplasm.
This gel is mostly water, but there are lots of proteins here too.
Proteins are made here in the endoplasmic reticulum.
And the golgi apparatus moves proteins around the cell.

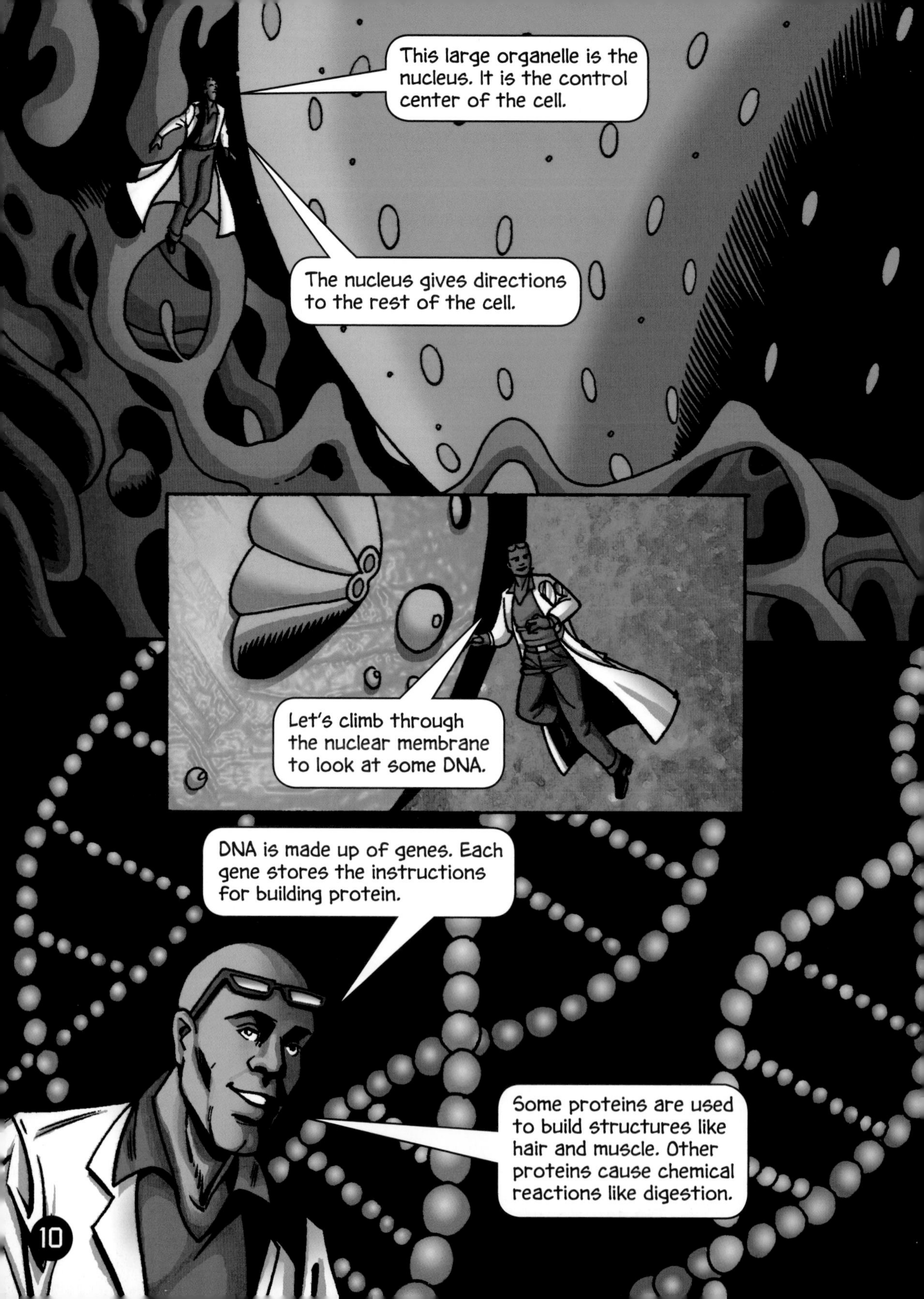
This large organelle is the nucleus. It is the control center of the cell.
The nucleus gives directions to the rest of the cell.
Let's climb through the nuclear membrane to look at some DNA.
DNA is made up of genes. Each gene stores the instructions for building protein.
Some proteins are used to build structures like hair and muscle. Other proteins cause chemical reactions like digestion.

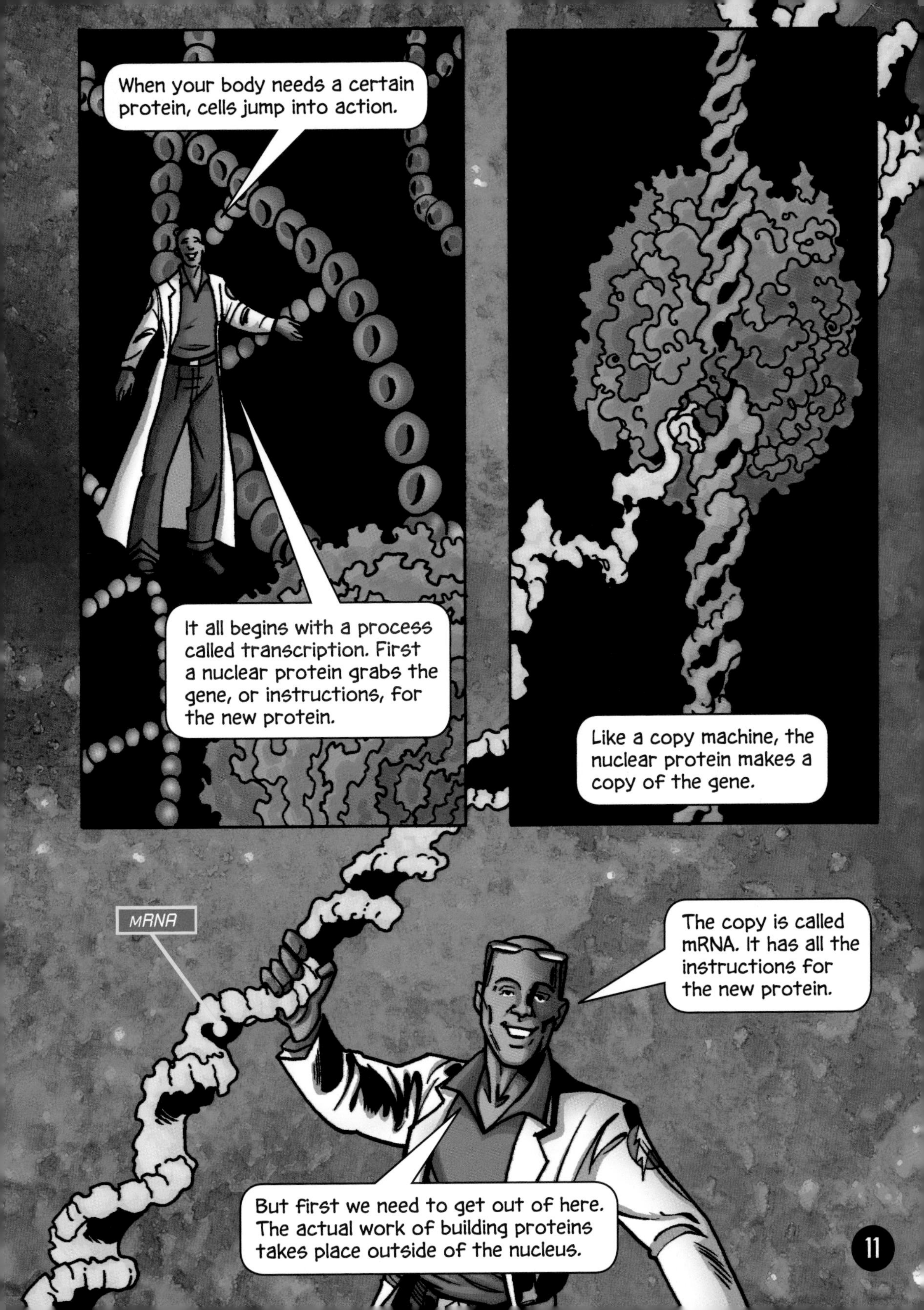
When your body needs a certain protein, cells jump into action.
It all begins with a process called transcription. First a nuclear protein grabs the gene, or instructions, for the new protein.
Like a copy machine, the nuclear protein makes a copy of the gene.
mRNA
The copy is called mRNA. It has all the instructions for the new protein.
But first we need to get out of here. The actual work of building proteins takes place outside of the nucleus.

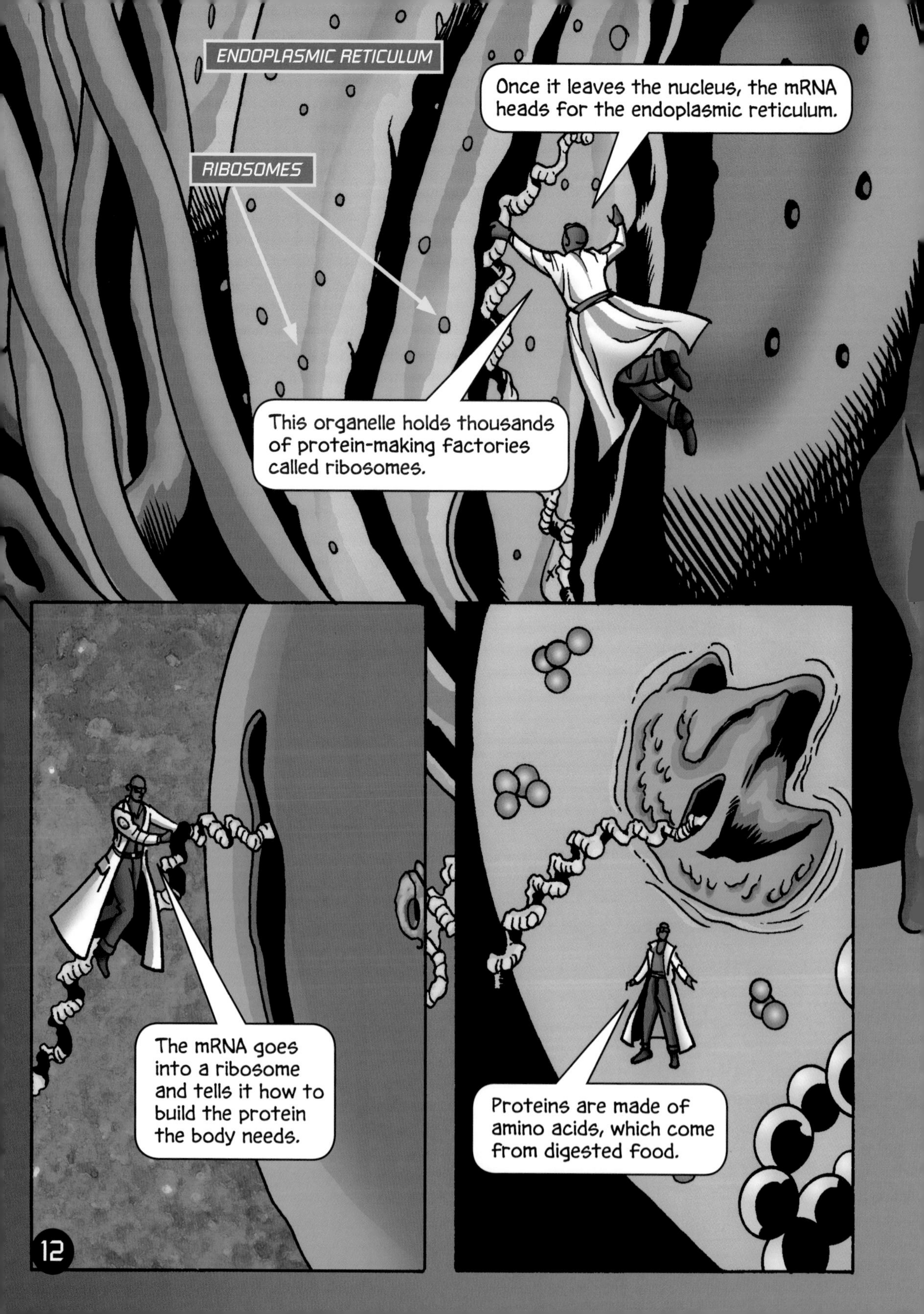
ENDOPLASMIC RETICULUM
RIBOSOMES
Once it leaves the nucleus, the mRNA heads for the endoplasmic reticulum.
This organelle holds thousands of protein-making factories called ribosomes.
The mRNA goes into a ribosome and tells it how to build the protein the body needs.
Proteins are made of amino acids, which come from digested food.

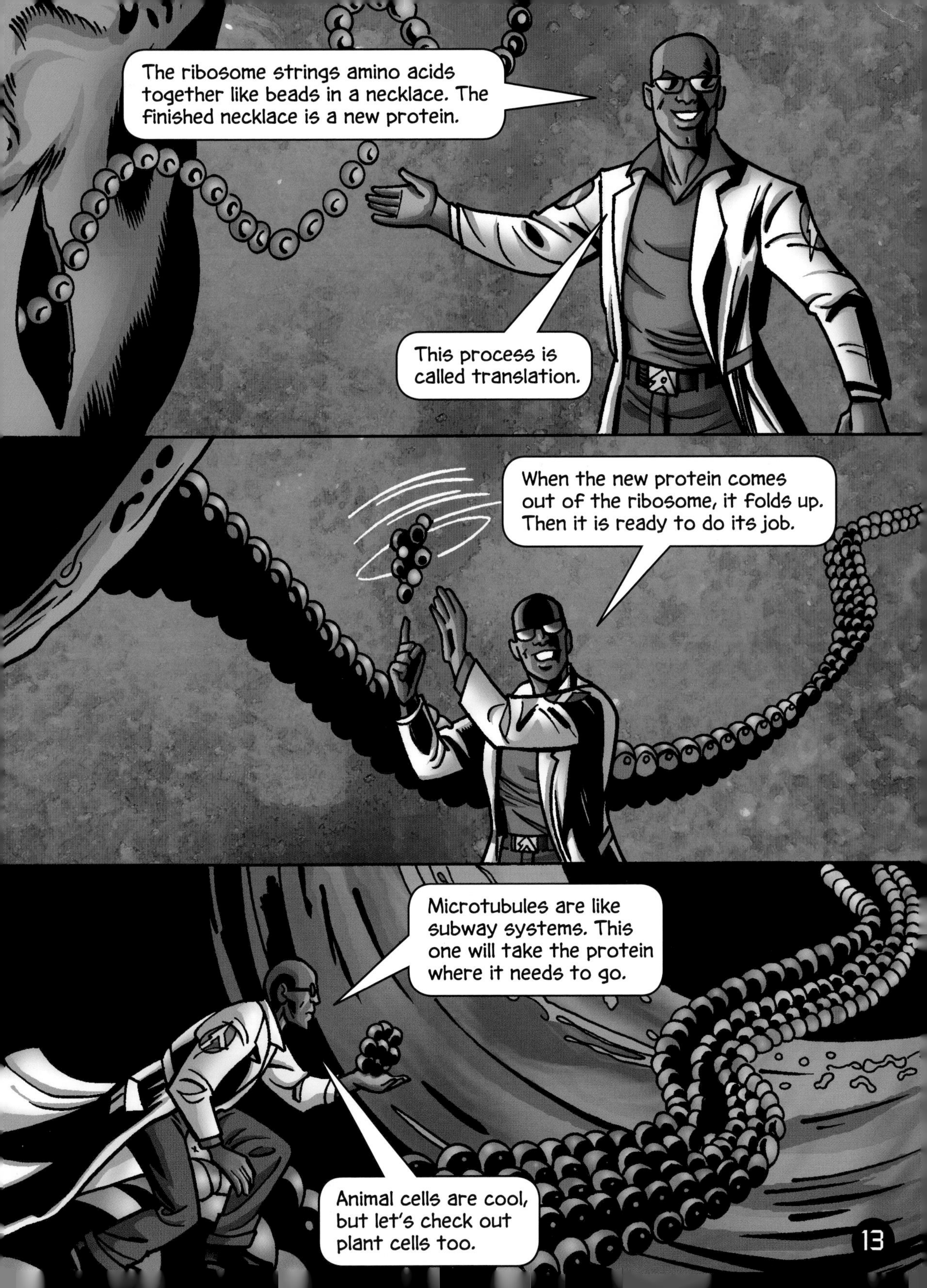
The ribosome strings amino acids together like beads in a necklace. The finished necklace is a new protein.
This process is called translation.
When the new protein comes out of the ribosome, it folds up. Then it is ready to do its job.
Microtubules are like subway systems. This one will take the protein where it needs to go.
Animal cells are cool, but let's check out plant cells too.

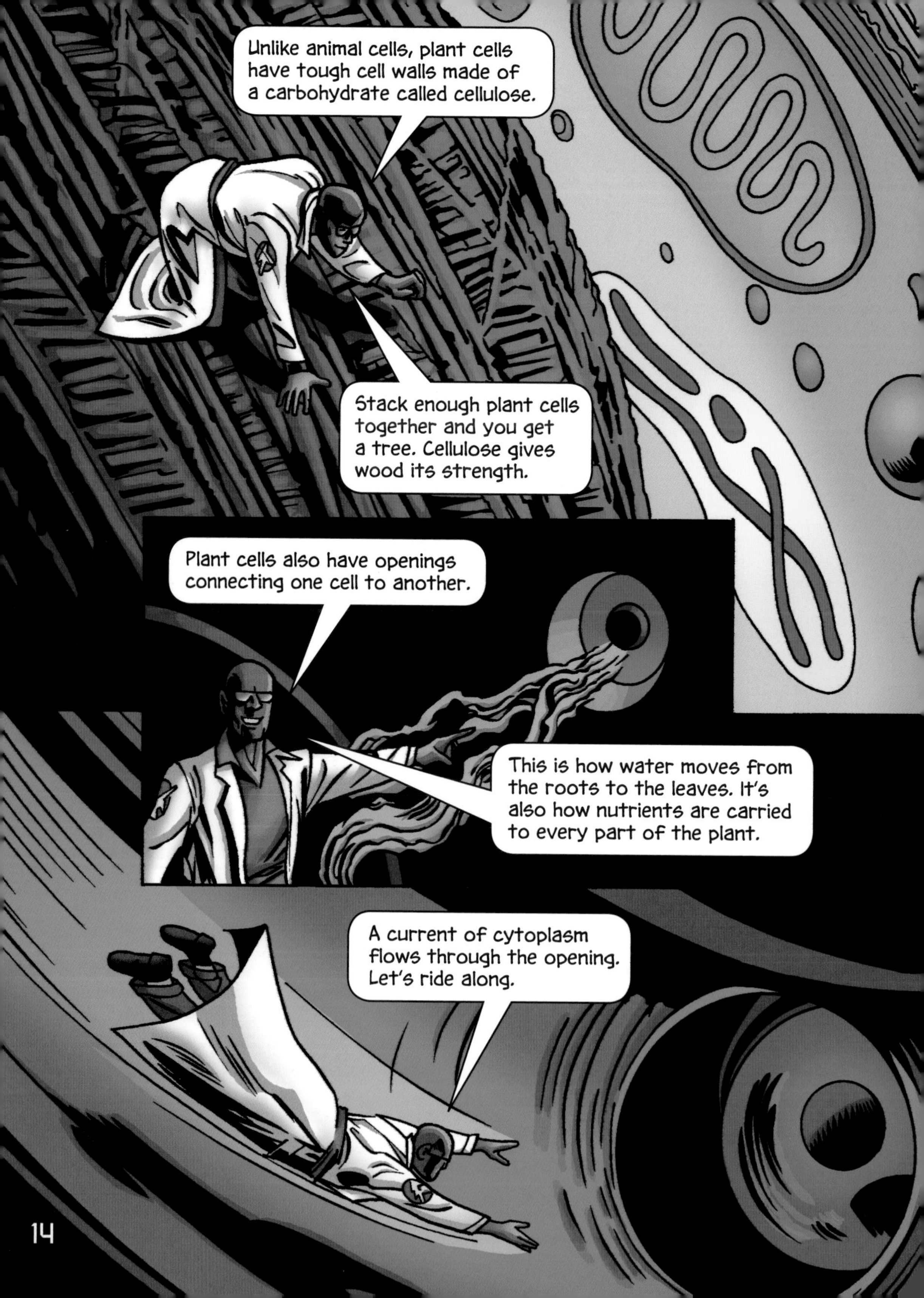
Unlike animal cells, plant cells have tough cell walls made of a carbohydrate called cellulose.
Stack enough plant cells together and you get a tree. Cellulose gives wood its strength.
Plant cells also have openings connecting one cell to another.
This is how water moves from the roots to the leaves. It's also how nutrients are carried to every part of the plant.
A current of cytoplasm flows through the opening. Let's ride along.

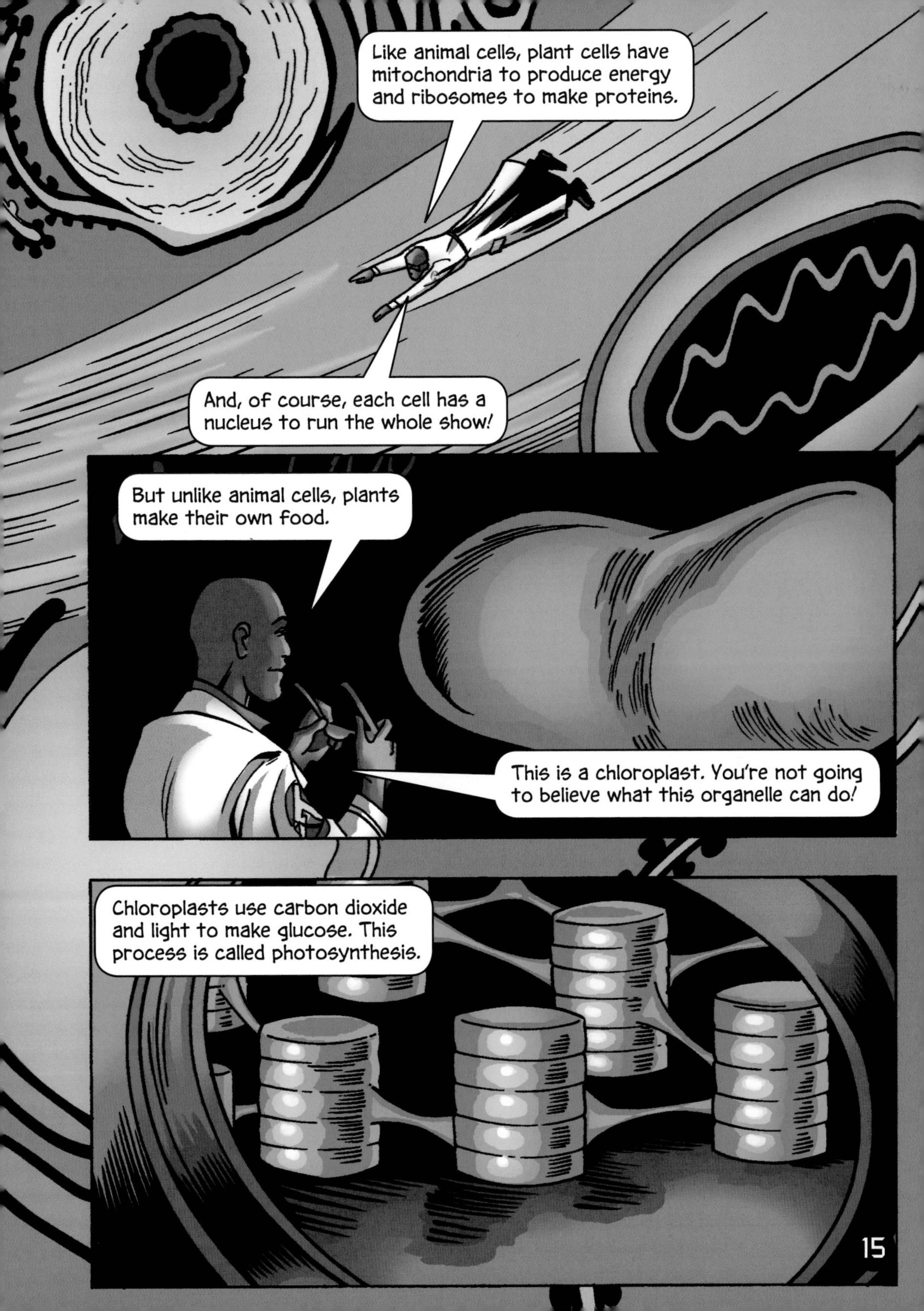
Like animal cells, plant cells have mitochondria to produce energy and ribosomes to make proteins.
And, of course, each cell has a nucleus to run the whole show!
But unlike animal cells, plants make their own food.
This is a chloroplast. You're not going to believe what this organelle can do!
Chloroplasts use carbon dioxide and light to make glucose. This process is called photosynthesis.

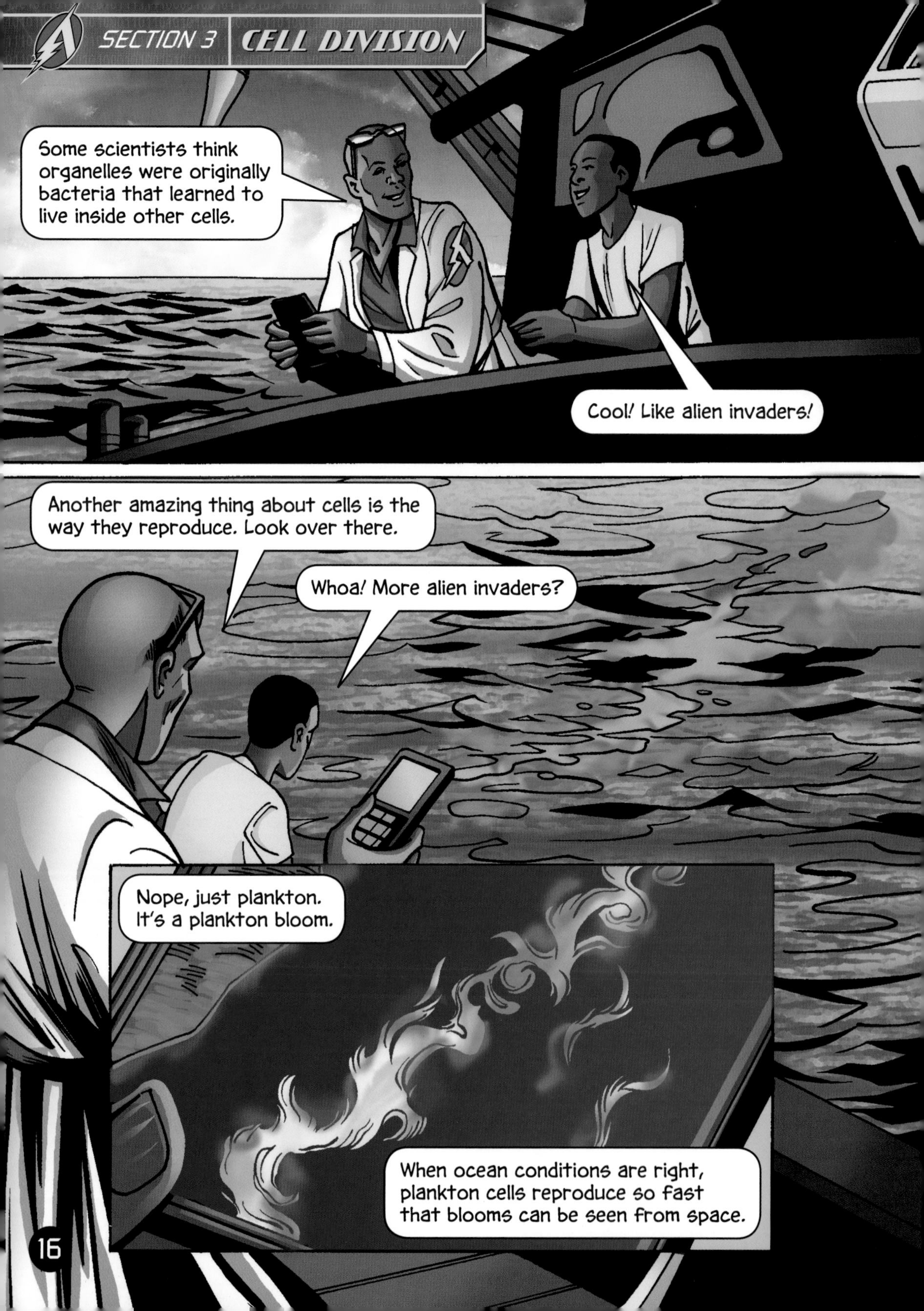
Some scientists think organelles were originally bacteria that learned to live inside other cells.
Cool! Like alien invaders!
Another amazing thing about cells is the way they reproduce. Look over there.
Whoa! More alien invaders?
Nope, just plankton. It's a plankton bloom.
When ocean conditions are right, plankton cells reproduce so fast that blooms can be seen from space.

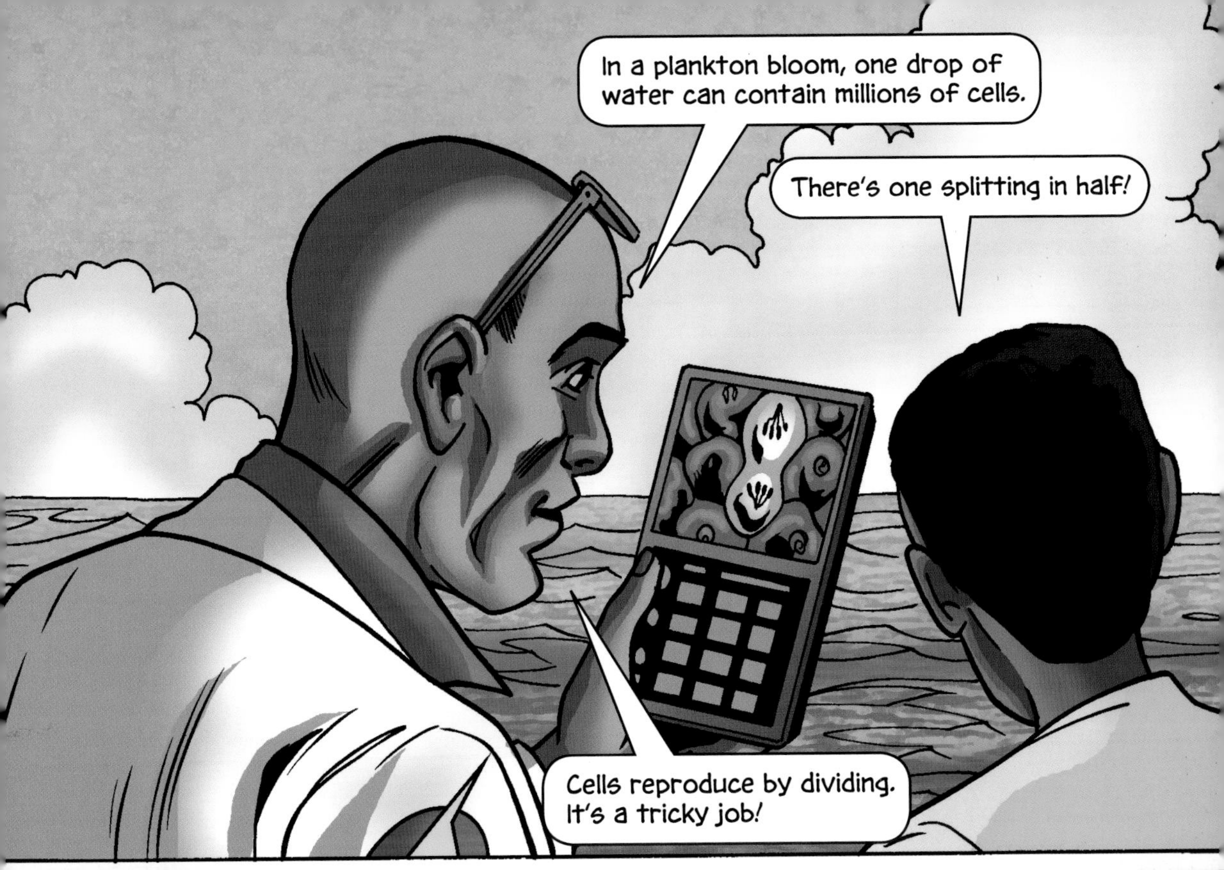
In a plankton bloom, one drop of water can contain millions of cells.
There's one splitting in half!
Cells reproduce by dividing. It's a tricky job!

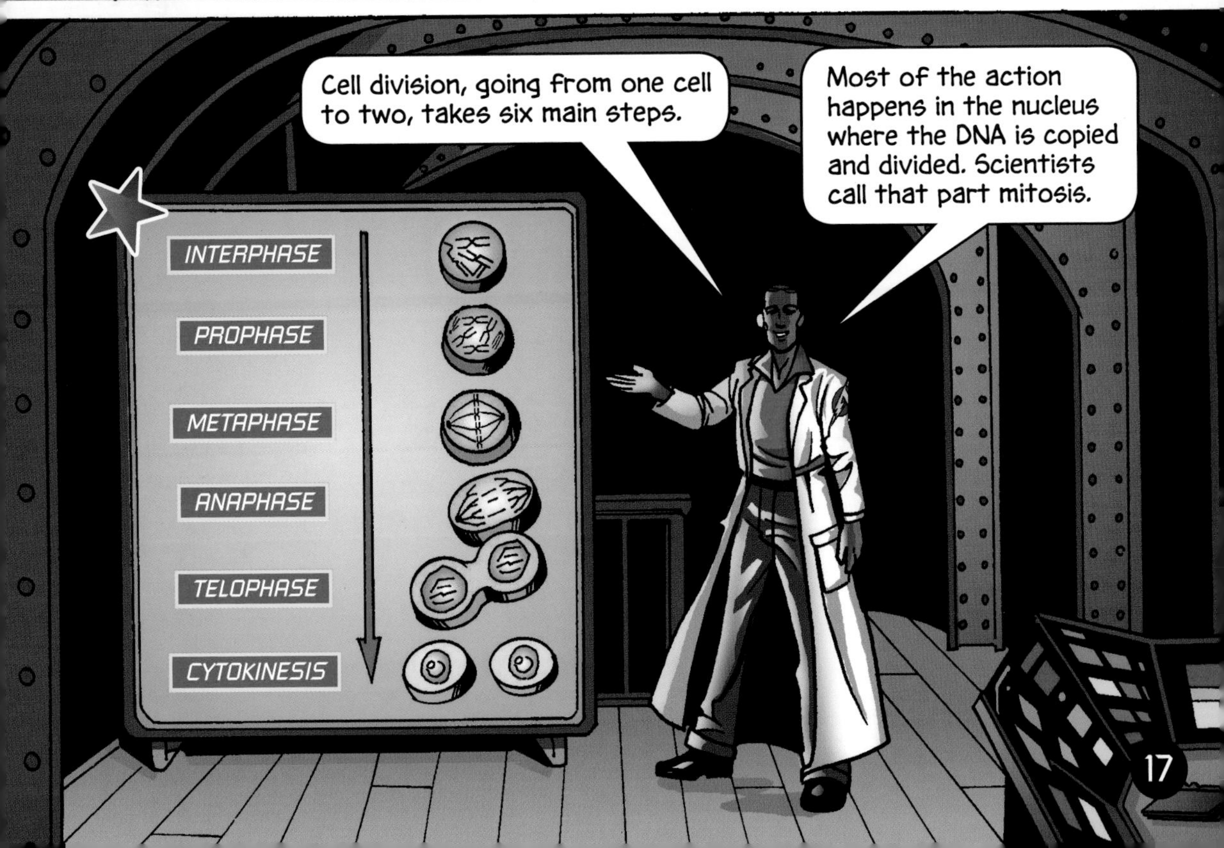
Cell division, going from one cell to two, takes six main steps.
Most of the action happens in the nucleus where the DNA is copied and divided. Scientists call that part mitosis.
INTERPHASE
PROPHASE
METAPHASE
ANAPHASE
TELOPHASE
CYTOKINESIS

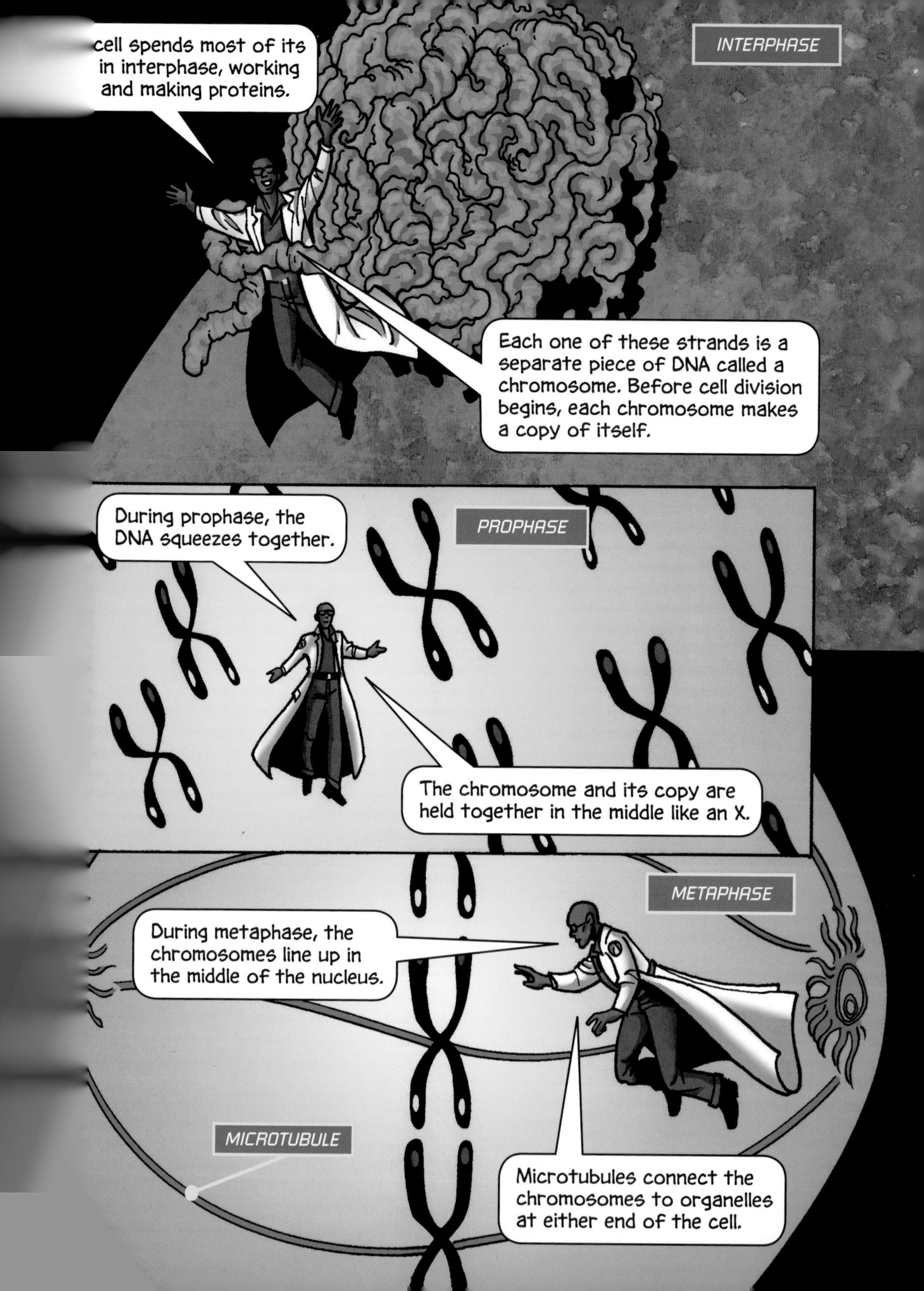
INTERPHASE
cell spends most of its in interphase, working and making proteins.
Each one of these strands is a separate piece of DNA called a chromosome. Before cell division begins, each chromosome makes a copy of itself.
PROPHASE
During prophase, the DNA squeezes together.
The chromosome and its copy are held together in the middle like an X.
METAPHASE
During metaphase, the chromosomes line up in the middle of the nucleus.
MICROTUBULE
Microtubules connect the chromosomes to organelles at either end of the cell.

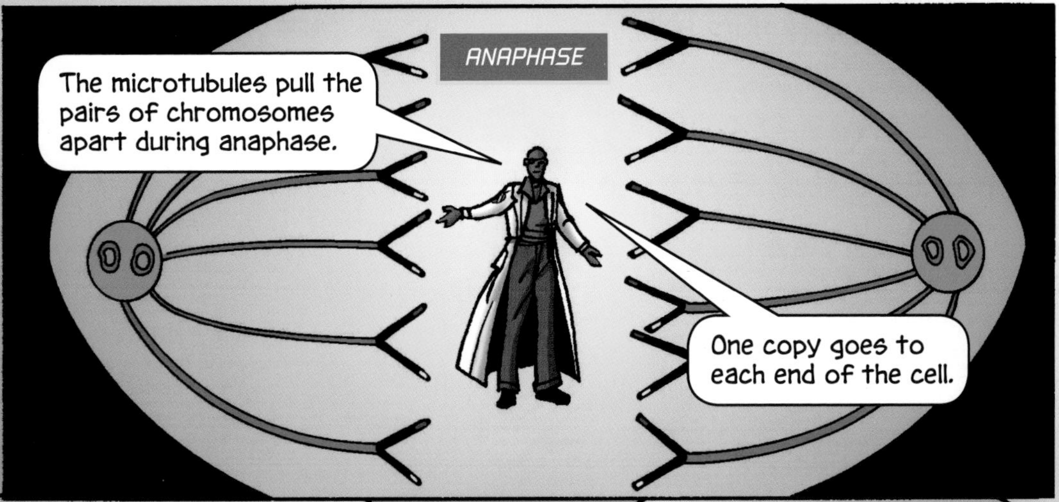
ANAPHASE
The microtubules pull the pairs of chromosomes apart during anaphase.
One copy goes to each end of the cell.

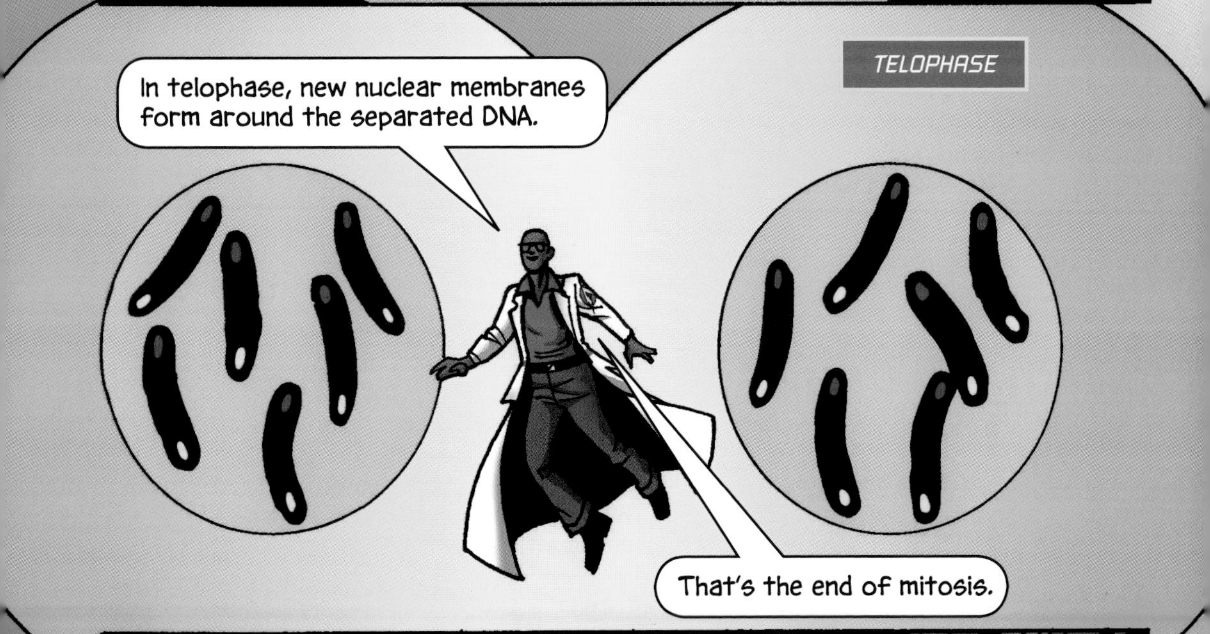
TELOPHASE
In telophase, new nuclear membranes form around the separated DNA.
That's the end of mitosis.

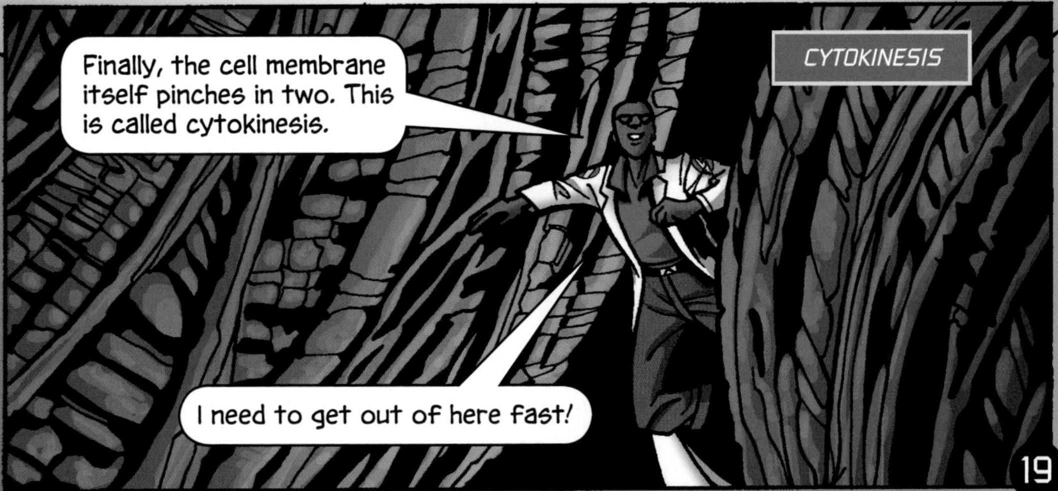
CYTOKINESIS
Finally, the cell membrane itself pinches in two. This is called cytokinesis.
I need to get out of here fast!

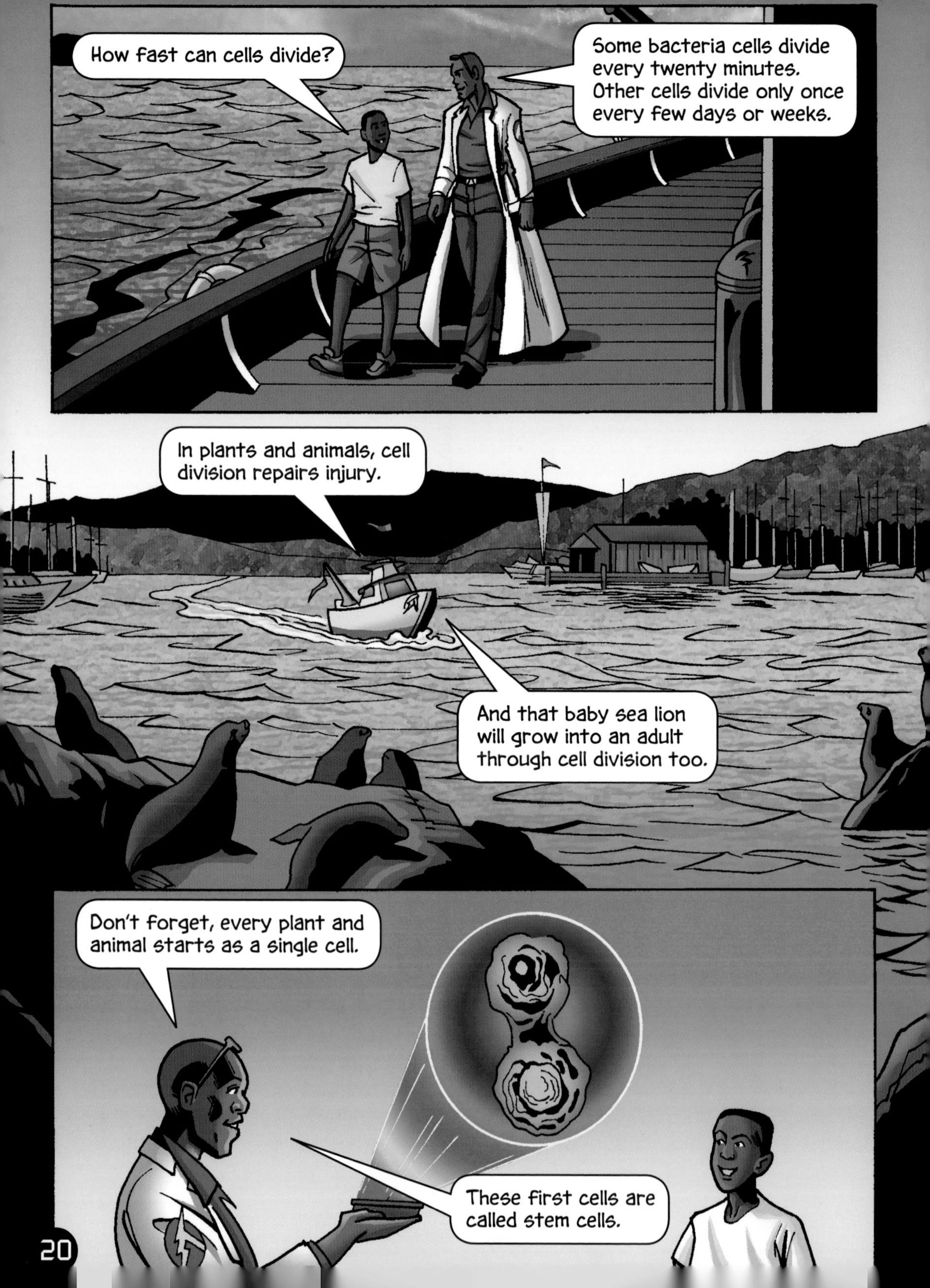
How fast can cells divide?
Some bacteria cells divide every twenty minutes. Other cells divide only once every few days or weeks.
In plants and animals, cell division repairs injury.
And that baby sea lion will grow into an adult through cell division too.
Don't forget, every plant and animal starts as a single cell.
These first cells are called stem cells.

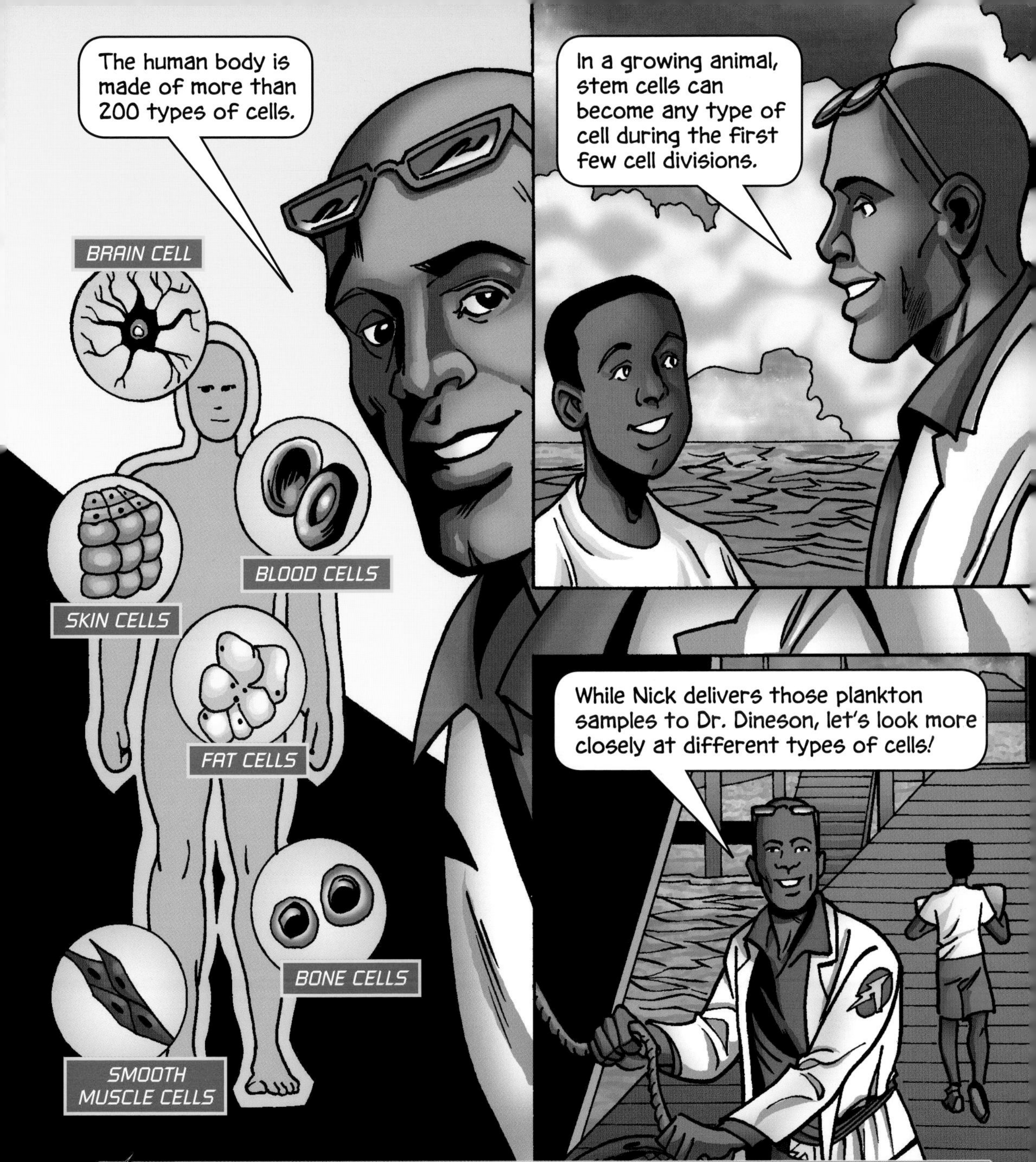
The human body is made of more than 200 types of cells.
BRAIN CELL
BLOOD CELLS
SKIN CELLS
FAT CELLS
BONE CELLS
SMOOTH MUSCLE CELLS
In a growing animal, stem cells can become any type of cell during the first few cell divisions.
While Nick delivers those plankton samples to Dr. Dineson, let's look more closely at different types of cells!

STEM CELLS IN MEDICINE

ACCESS GRANTED: MAX AXIOM

Scientists think that stem cells may be the answer to curing many diseases such as Parkinson's or Alzheimer's. Doctors may be able to use stem cells to replace old cells damaged by injury or disease. Bone marrow transplants are a form of stem cell therapy used to treat cancers like leukemia and lymphoma.

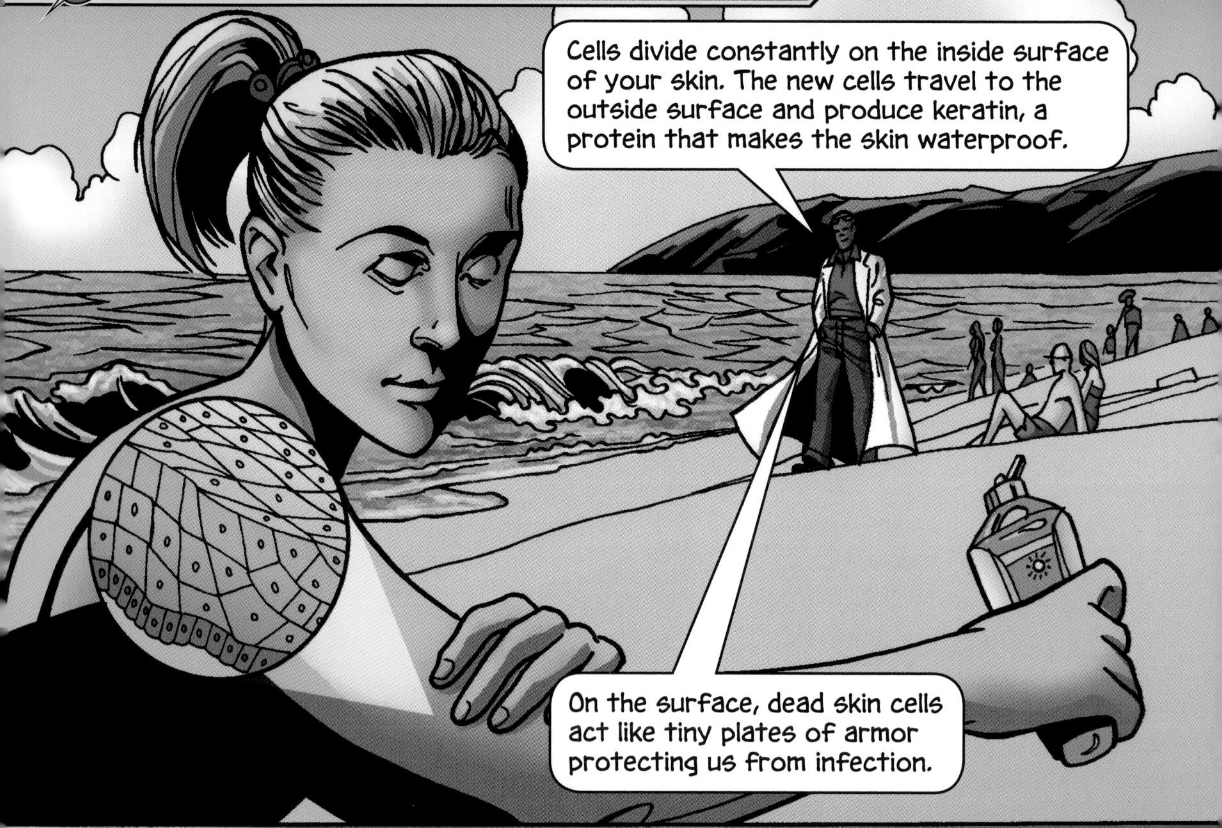
Cells divide constantly on the inside surface of your skin. The new cells travel to the outside surface and produce keratin, a protein that makes the skin waterproof.
On the surface, dead skin cells act like tiny plates of armor protecting us from infection.

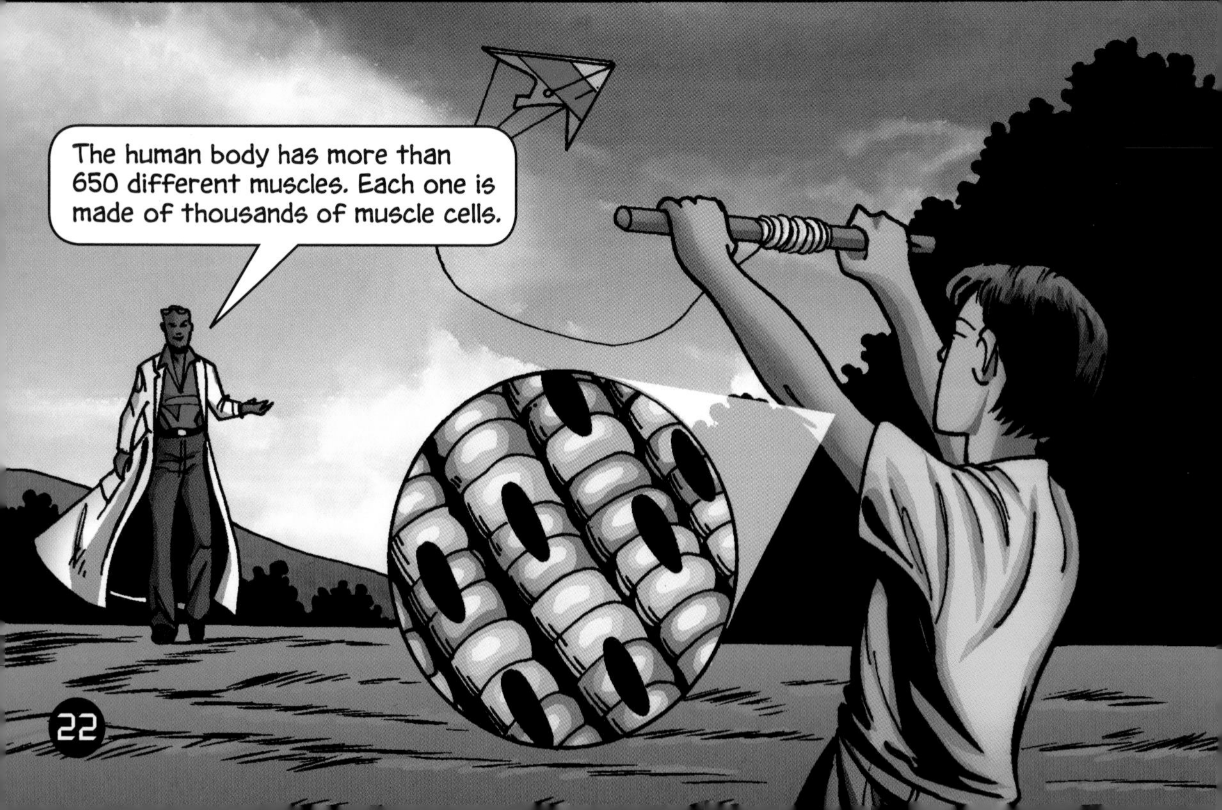
The human body has more than 650 different muscles. Each one is made of thousands of muscle cells.

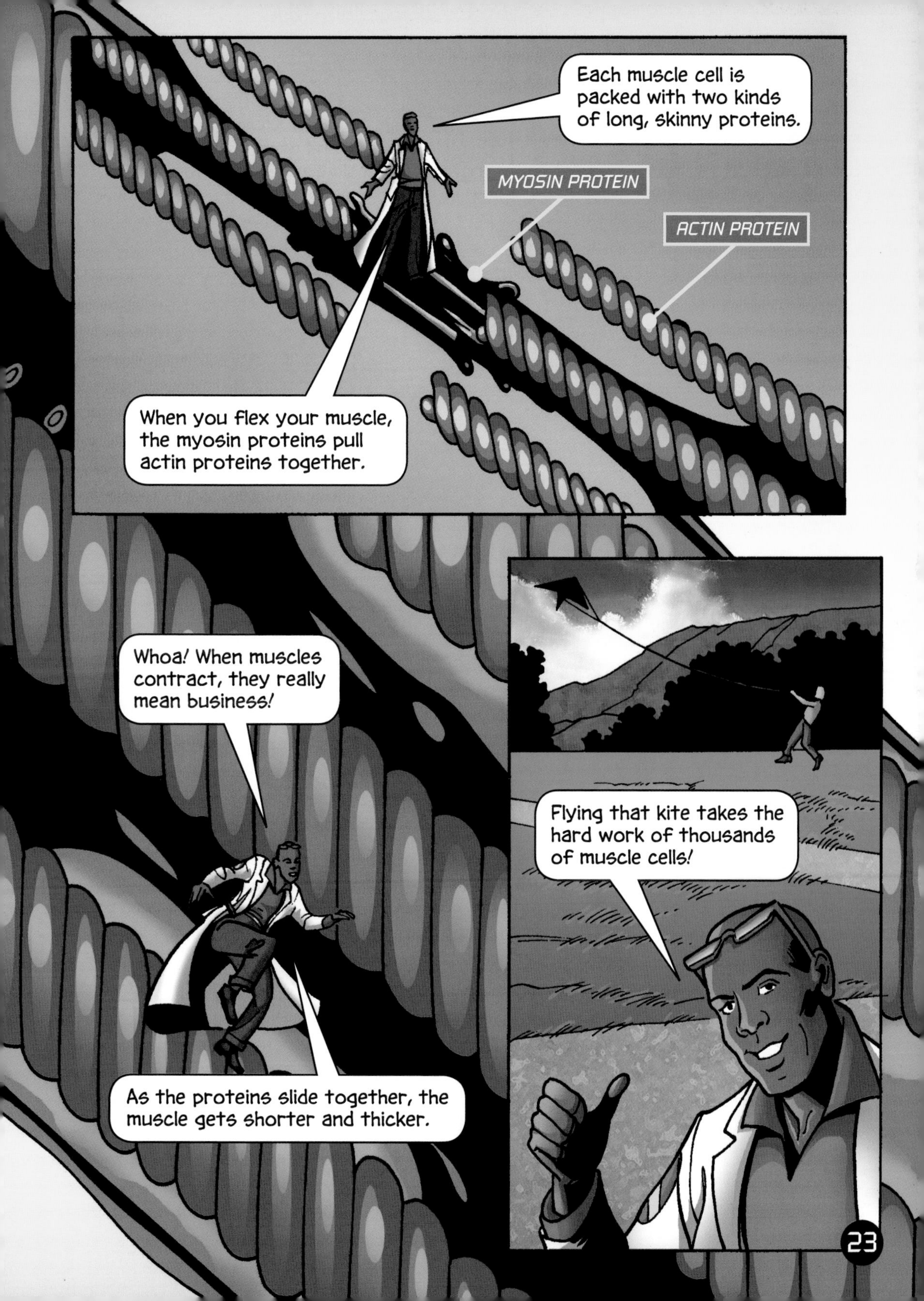
Each muscle cell is packed with two kinds of long, skinny proteins.
MYOSIN PROTEIN
ACTIN PROTEIN
When you flex your muscle, the myosin proteins pull actin proteins together.
Whoa! When muscles contract, they really mean business!
As the proteins slide together, the muscle gets shorter and thicker.
Flying that kite takes the hard work of thousands of muscle cells!

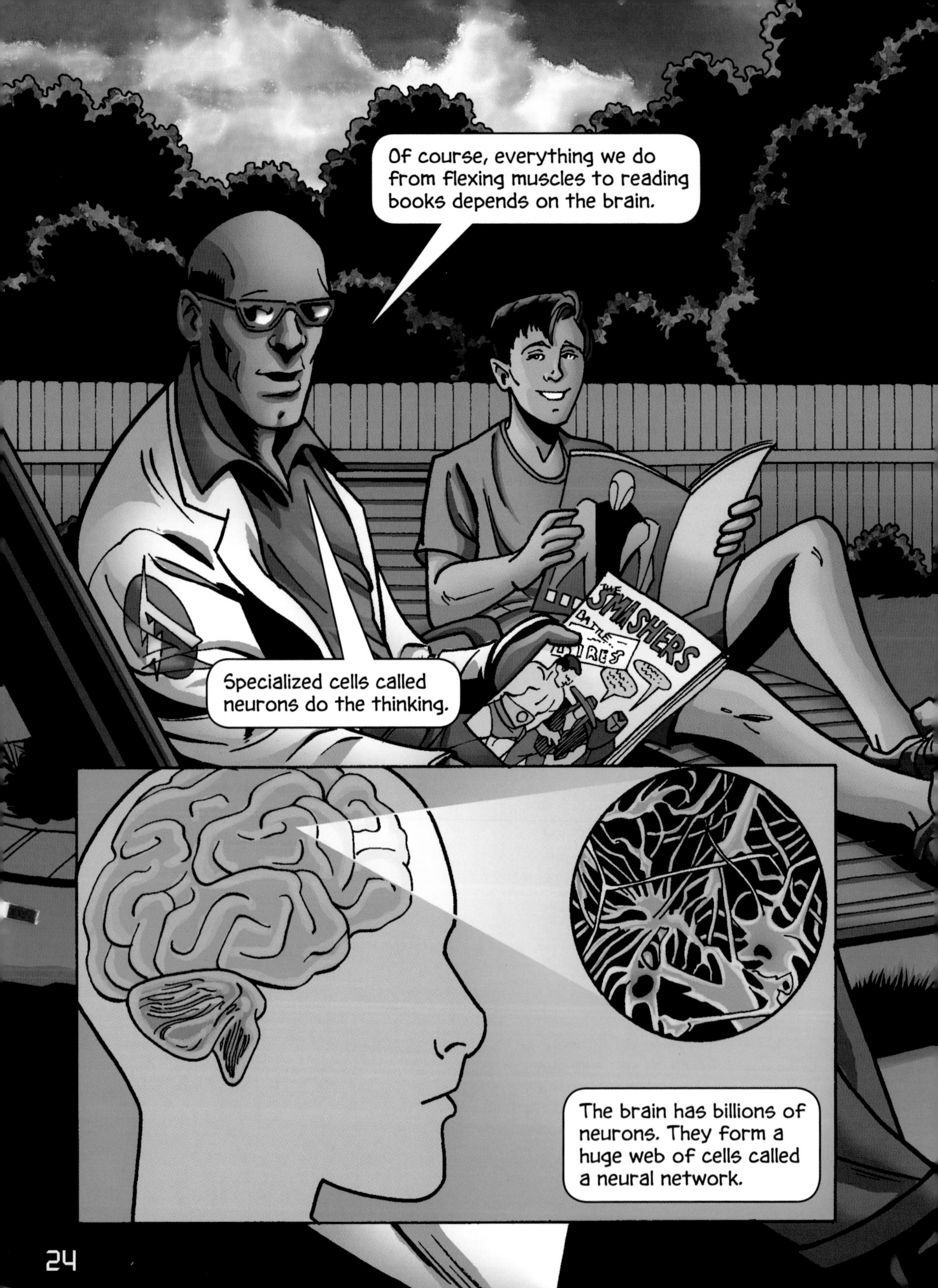
Of course, everything we do from flexing muscles to reading books depends on the brain.
Specialized cells called neurons do the thinking.
The brain has billions of neurons. They form a huge web of cells called a neural network.

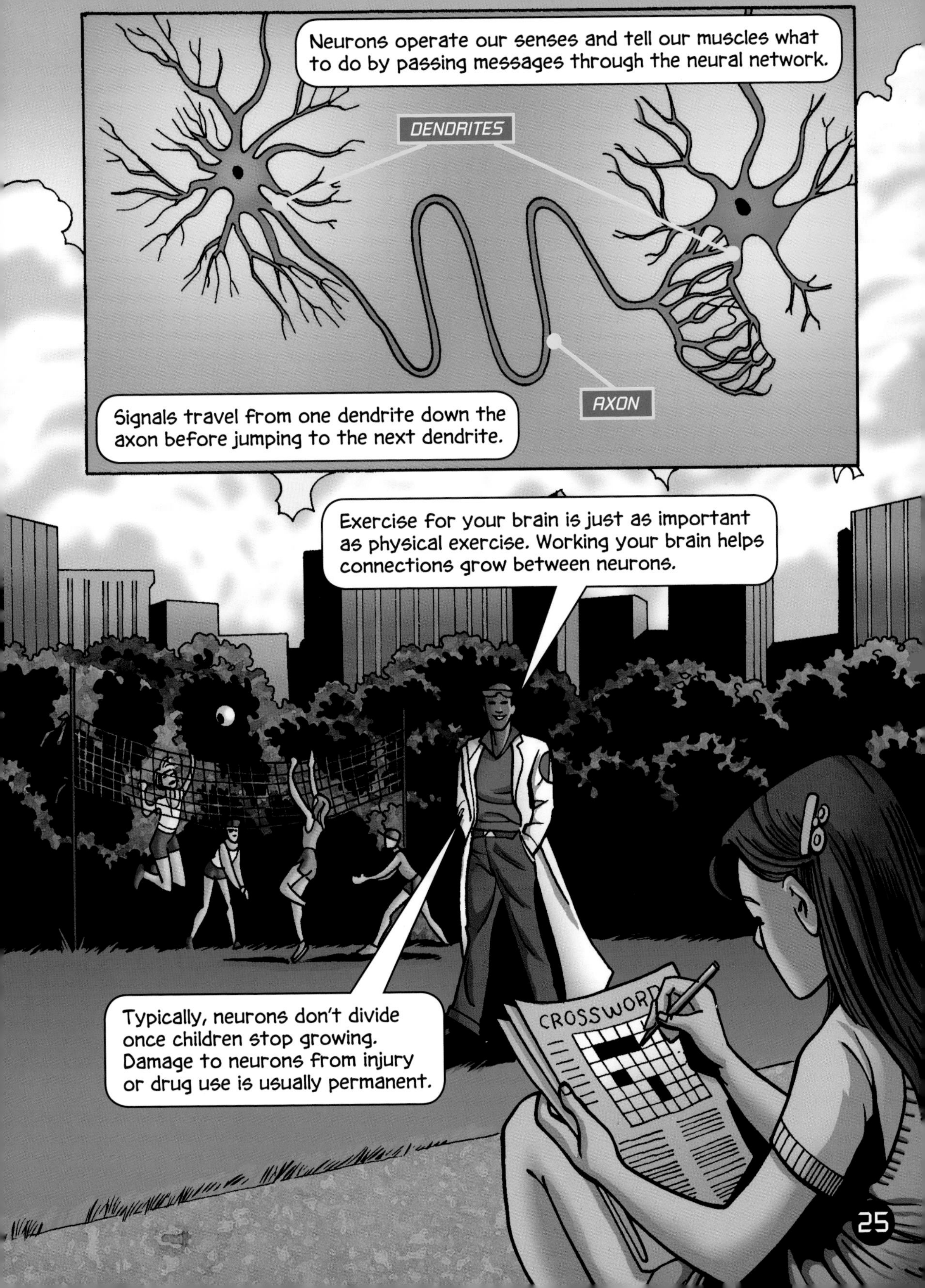
Neurons operate our senses and tell our muscles what to do by passing messages through the neural network.
DENDRITES
AXON
Signals travel from one dendrite down the axon before jumping to the next dendrite.
Exercise for your brain is just as important as physical exercise. Working your brain helps connections grow between neurons.
Typically, neurons don't divide once children stop growing. Damage to neurons from injury or drug use is usually permanent.
CROSSWORD

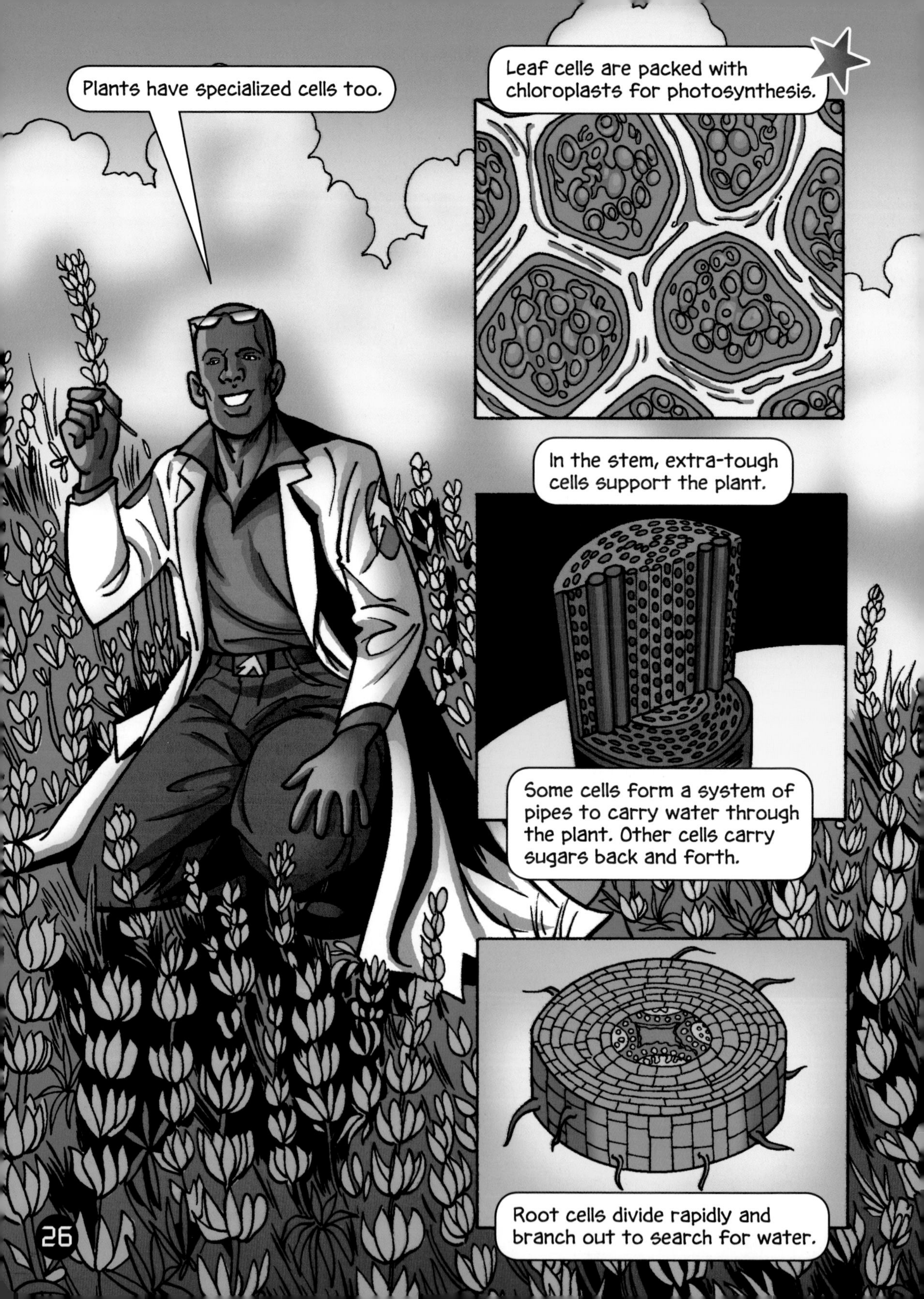
Plants have specialized cells too.
Leaf cells are packed with chloroplasts for photosynthesis.
In the stem, extra-tough cells support the plant.
Some cells form a system of pipes to carry water through the plant. Other cells carry sugars back and forth.
Root cells divide rapidly and branch out to search for water.

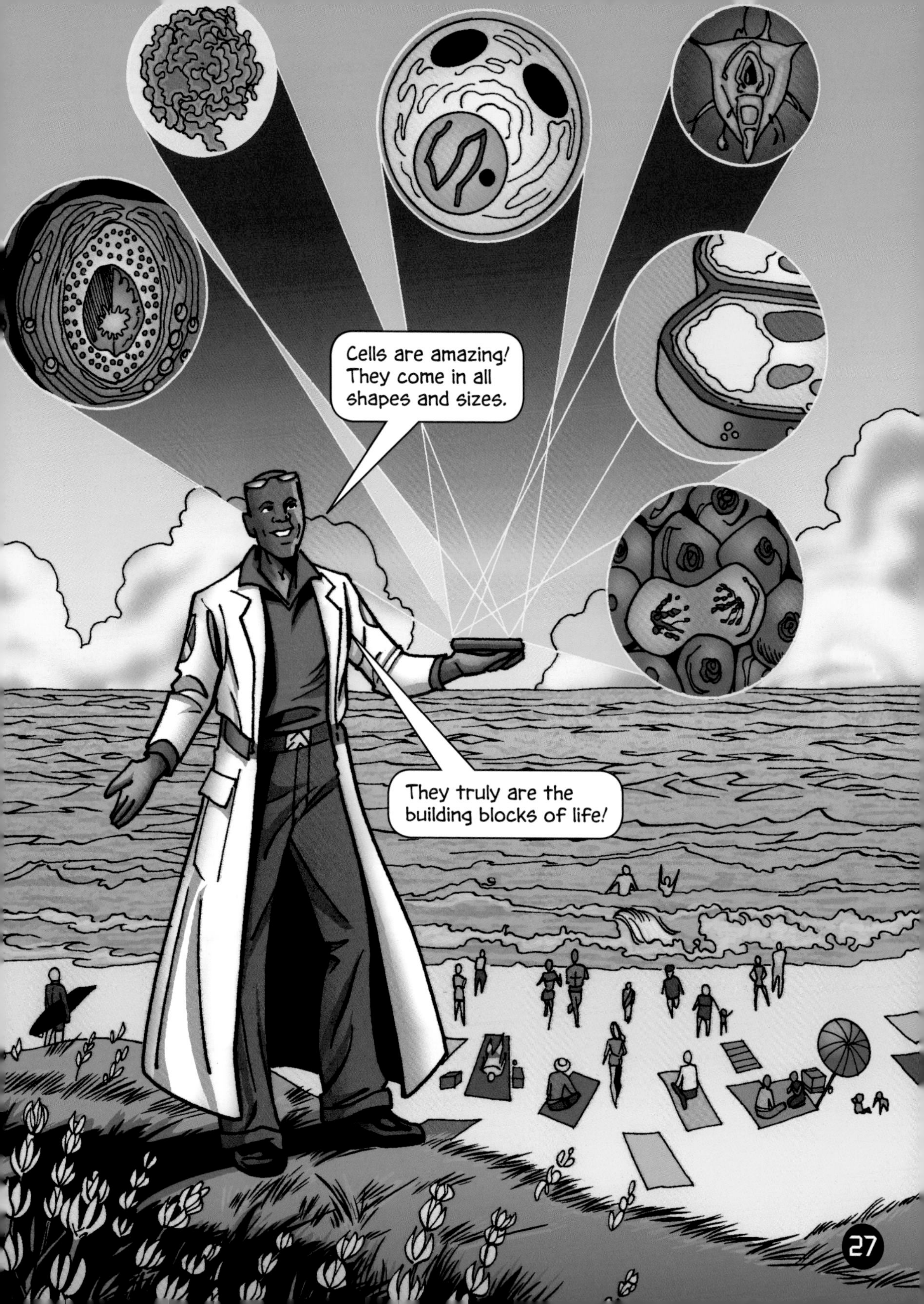
Cells are amazing! They come in all shapes and sizes.
They truly are the building blocks of life!

Robert Hooke discovered cells in 1665 when he used a microscope to examine thin slices of cork. He saw tiny boxes that looked like the rooms where monks lived. Those rooms were called cells. Hooke gave that name to his discovery.

In 1683, Anton van Leeuwenhoek built a microscope to observe bacteria found in his own mouth. He called them animalcules.

In 1839, scientists Matthias Schleiden and Theodor Schwann convinced the world that all living things are made of cells. An important part of cell theory is that all cells come from the division of other cells.

All cells are tiny, but they come in different shapes and sizes. The largest cells are found in frog eggs. They are nearly 0.04 inches (1 millimeter) in diameter.

Neurobiology, the study of the brain, is an exciting area of medical research. Scientists use Magnetic Resonance Imaging, or MRI, to take pictures of active neurons. These color photos show which parts of the brain are active when a person plays music or solves crossword puzzles.

Cell division is a complicated process. Damage to cells may cause them to divide and reproduce incorrectly. When this happens, cells grow in places they shouldn't. The resulting disease is called cancer.

One tool biologists use to study cells is called a cell culture. A cell culture is a sample of cells that is kept alive in the laboratory through continuous cell division.

Dehydration is more dangerous than starvation because the cytoplasm of cells is made mostly of water. Without water, nothing inside the cell will work correctly. Humans can survive without eating for much longer than they can go without water because cells can use energy stored in fat cells.

ANIMAL CELL-O

Learn all about the parts of an animal cell by building a model that's good enough to eat!

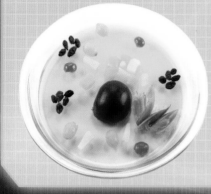

WHAT YOU NEED:

- Internet access
- paper and pencil
- lemon gelatin mix
- saucepan
- spoon
- pie plate
- can opener
- can of fruit cocktail
- strainer
- paring knife
- cutting board
- plum
- apple
- raisins

WHAT YOU DO:

1. Use the Internet to find a labeled cross-section diagram of an animal cell. Draw a picture of the diagram and include the labels for future reference.

2. With an adult's help, make the gelatin according to the box's instructions, but with about ¾ of the water recommended.

3. Pour the gelatin into the pie plate. The pie plate represents the cell membrane and the gelatin represents the cytoplasm.

4. Place the gelatin in the refrigerator to cool for about 45 minutes.

5. While the gelatin cools, open and drain the can of fruit cocktail, cut the plum in half, and peel the apple's skin into a long, thin strip.

6. Remove the gelatin from the refrigerator. Then use your diagram from step 1 to add organelles to the cell model with your fruit supplies. Use half of the plum as the nucleus and cluster peach and pear chunks near it to represent the rough and smooth endoplasmic reticulum.

7. Continue adding organelles to your model. Pineapple chunks can serve as vacuoles, cherries as lysosomes, grapes as mitochondria, a peach chunk as the centrosome, and clusters of raisins as ribosomes.

8. Lastly, fold the apple skin into an accordion shape and add it to your model as golgi bodies.

9. Refrigerate your animal cell model for several hours. Then show it off and serve it to your friends and classmates! Yum!

DISCUSSION QUESTIONS

1. The two main kinds of cells are prokaryotic cells and eukaryotic cells. How are these two types of cells alike? How are they different? Explain your answers.

2. What does the term "organelle" remind you of? Why do you think scientists use it to refer to the main parts of a cell?

3. Compare and contrast plant and animal cells. What features do they have in common? What features make them different?

4. Why do organisms need specialized cells? What are some of the specialized cells in the human body, and what do they do?

WRITING PROMPTS

1. In section 2, Max describes how animal cells use energy to make proteins in a process called metabolism. Review pages 8 to 13 and create a flow chart that shows the main steps of this process.

2. Cell division has six main steps. Make a list of these steps and use the illustrations on pages 17 through 19 to draw your own pictures of what happens during each one.

3. Imagine that you could shrink down to go inside a plant or animal cell like Max. Write a short story in which you do so. Describe what you do and what you see while you're inside the cell.

4. The human body has more than 200 types of cells. Pick one mentioned in this book and research it online. Then write a short paragraph explaining why that type of cell is so important.

TAKE A QUIZ!

READ MORE

Anders, Mason. *Animal Cells*. Genetics. North Mankato, Minn.: Capstone Press, 2018.

Hand, Carol. *Cell Theory: The Structure and Function of Cells*. Great Discoveries in Science. New York: Cavendish Square, 2019.

Lomberg, Michelle. *Animal Cells*. Nature of Life. New York: Smartbook Media, Inc., 2017.

Paris, Stephanie Herweck. *Cells*. Huntington Beach, Calif.: Teacher Created Materials, 2016.

INTERNET SITES

Use Facthound to find Internet sites related to this book.

Visit www.facthound.com

Just type in 9781543558753 and go!

Super-cool stuff! Check out projects, games and lots more at www.capstonekids.com

INDEX

amino acid (uh-MEE-noh ASS-id)—a basic building block of protein that contains nitrogen; amino acids can be made by the body or ingested through eating foods with protein

ATP (AY TEE PEE)—a molecule that provides energy to cells

cellulose (SEL-yuh-lohss)—the substance from which the cell walls of plants are made

DNA (DEE EN AY)—the genetic material that carries all of the instructions to make a living thing and keep it working; DNA stands for deoxyribonucleic acid

gene (JEEN)—a part of every cell that carries physical and behavioral information passed from parents to their children

glucose (GLOO-kose)—a natural sugar found in plants that gives energy to living things

metabolism (muh-TAB-uh-liz-uhm)—the process of changing food into energy

mitosis (mye-TOE-sis)—the process of cell division where one nucleus divides into two creating two identical cells

organelle (or-guh-NELL)—a small structure in a cell that performs a specific function and is surrounded by its own membrane

photosynthesis (foh-toh-SIN-thuh-siss)—the process by which green plants make their food

plankton (PLANGK-tuhn)—microscopic plants and animals that live in water

stem cell (STEM SELL)—a cell from which other types of cells can develop